Audio Access Included

Bach Two-Part Inventions
FOR MANDOLIN & GUITAR
ARRANGED BY CARLO AONZO AND JOHN CARLINI

To access audio visit:
www.halleonard.com/mylibrary
Enter Code
2935-9773-8767-8247

ISBN 978-1-4803-7211-5

HAL•LEONARD®
CORPORATION
7777 W. BLUEMOUND RD. P.O. BOX 13819 MILWAUKEE, WI 53213

In Australia Contact:
Hal Leonard Australia Pty. Ltd.
4 Lentara Court
Cheltenham, Victoria, 3192 Australia
Email: ausadmin@halleonard.com.au

Visit Hal Leonard Online at
www.halleonard.com

Contents

All arrangements by Carlo Aonzo and John Carlini.

Recorded, mixed, and mastered by Bob Harris at Ampersand Studios, Bridgewater, NJ.

Photography by Brian Glassman.

Introduction

Recording the 15 Bach Two-Part Inventions was a joyful experience!

We think that just a few words of explanation are appropriate here.

These keyboard studies were composed by Bach and completed in the 1720s. We have kept them in their original keys and arranged the right hand part for the mandolin and the left hand part for the guitar. Essentially, any two treble clef instruments could enjoy playing these arrangements.

Baroque "ornamentation" is a study in itself. We have used basically two types, the trill and the mordent. There is a wealth of information on ornaments available from many sources including the internet, but we think that by watching the music as you listen to the recording you will be able to see how they apply. And, of course, there is an abundance of recorded sources.

There are a few instances of repeated sections that Bach did not indicate, but we felt that they were natural for our project. On the recording there are a few notes on the guitar part that are lower than the 6th string E. In these instances, you are welcome to tune the 6th string to D to achieve the same effect, but we have notated those notes in the octave higher so that re-tuning is not necessary.

The tablature provided is only suggested. If you find a more comfortable location on the fingerboard to play phrases we encourage you to do so.

Enjoy this great music!

John Carlini and Carlo Aonzo

Invention No. 1

by Johann Sebastian Bach

Mandolin

Guitar

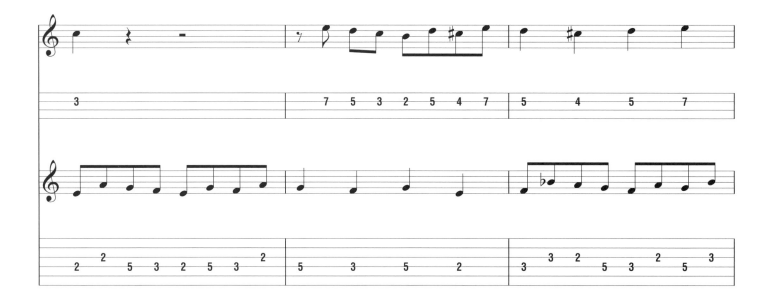

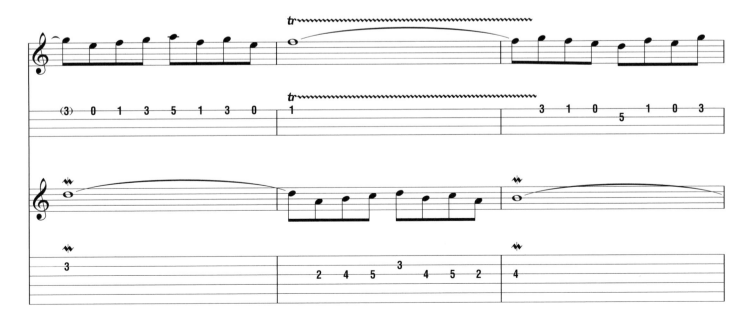

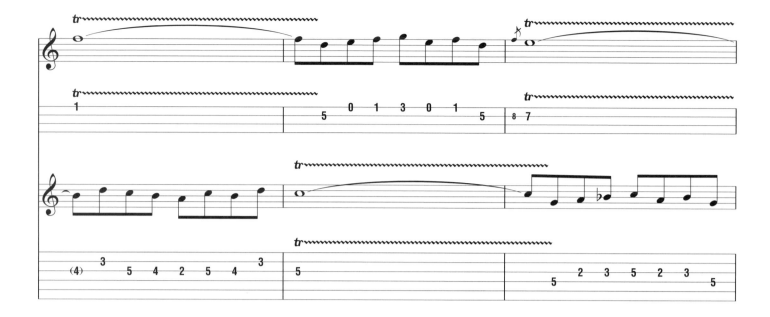

Invention No. 2

by Johann Sebastian Bach

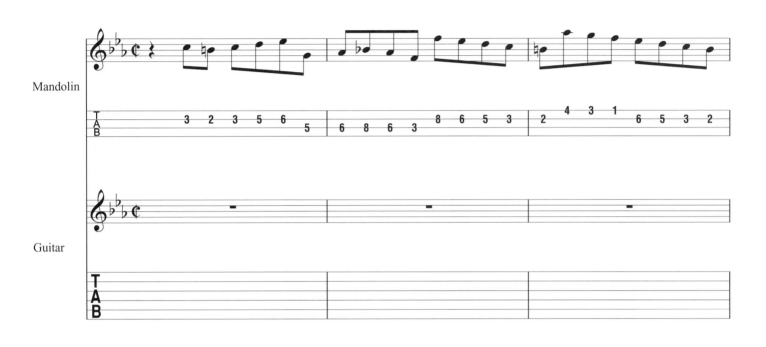

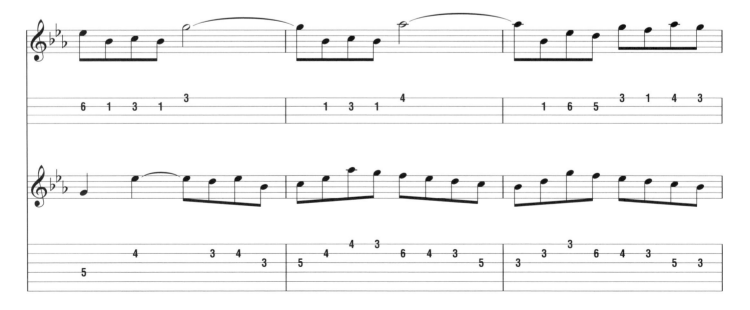

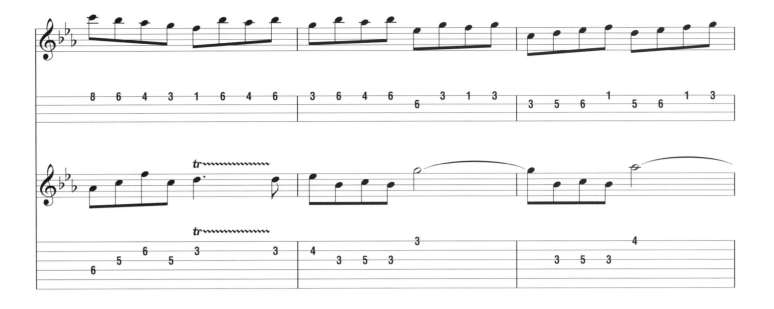

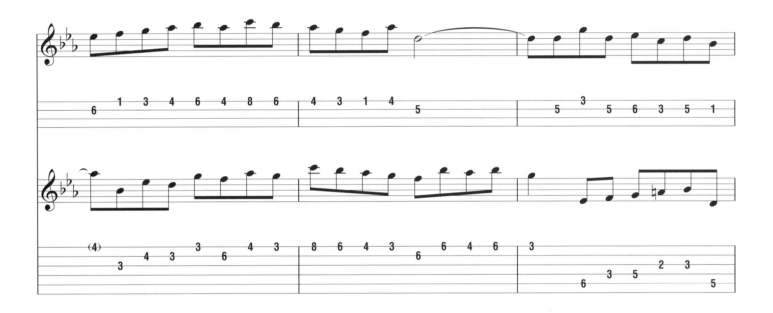

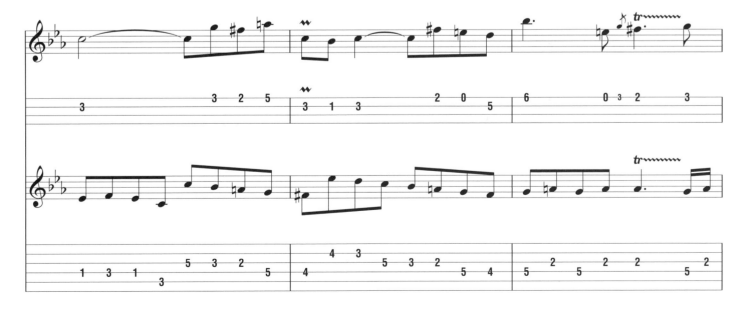

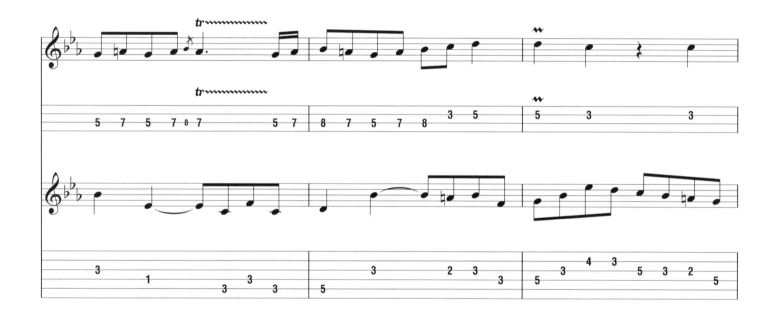

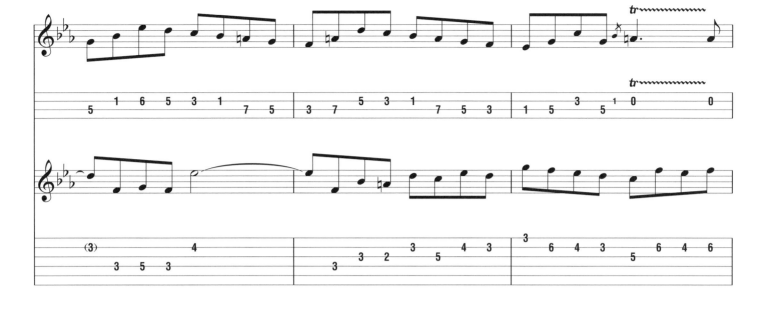

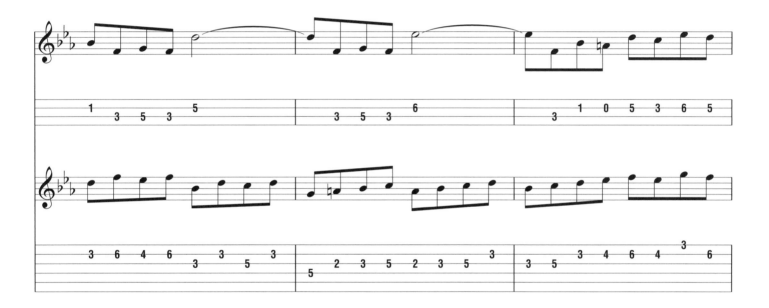

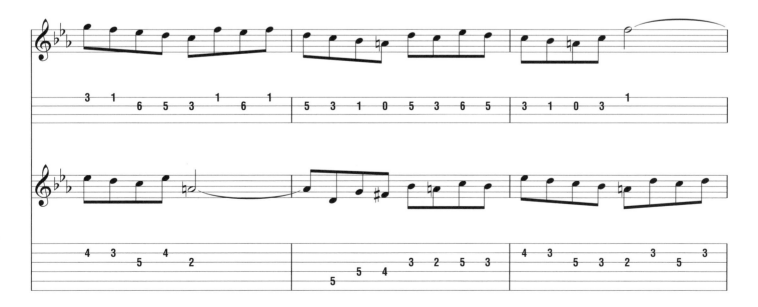

Invention No. 3

by Johann Sebastian Bach

Invention No. 4

by Johann Sebastian Bach

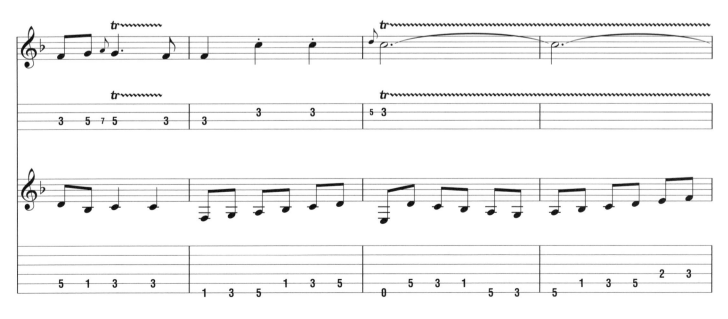

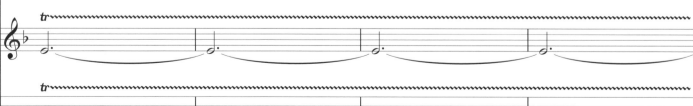

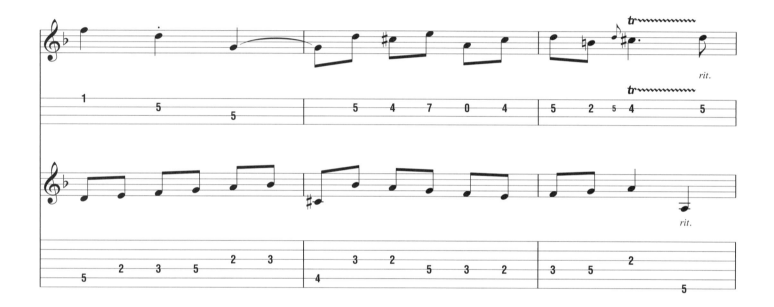

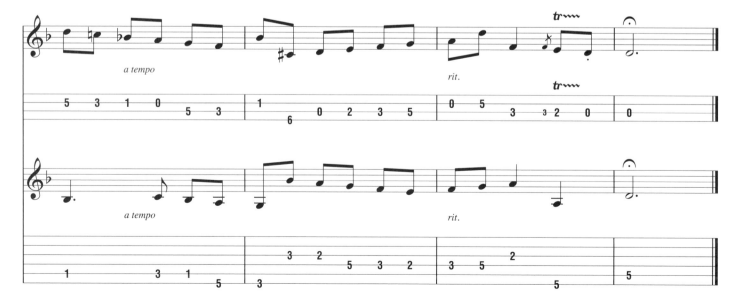

Invention No. 5

by Johann Sebastian Bach

Mandolin

Guitar

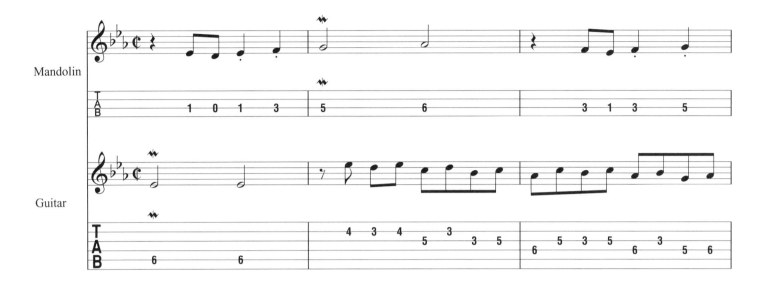

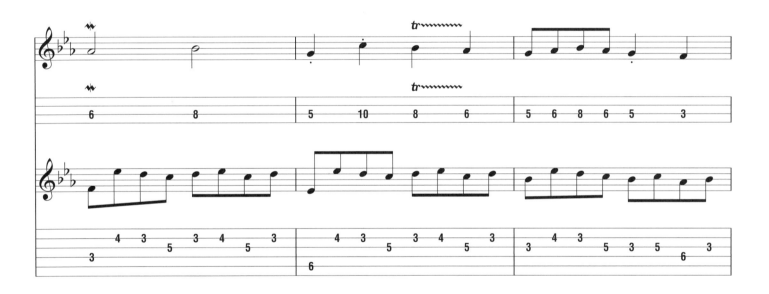

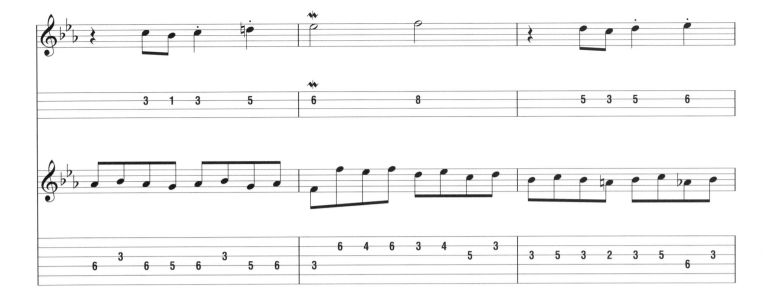

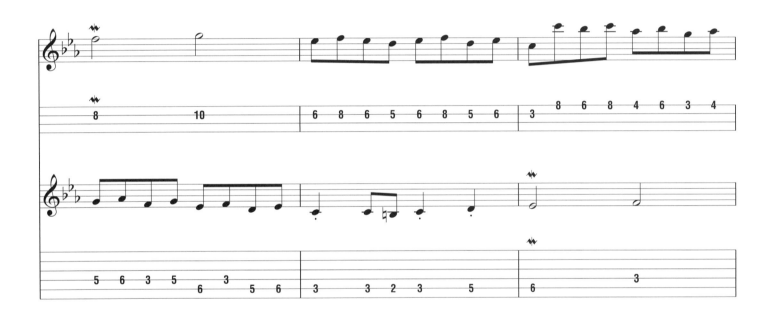

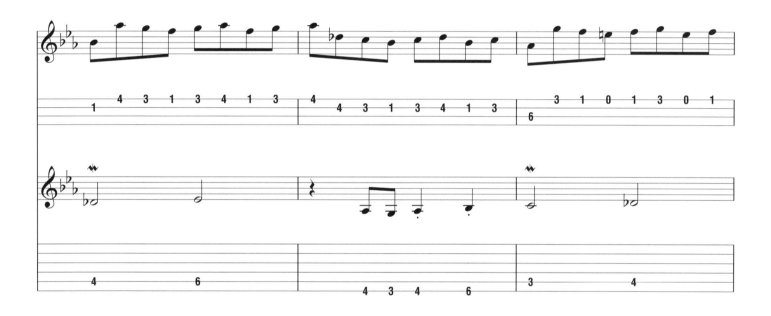

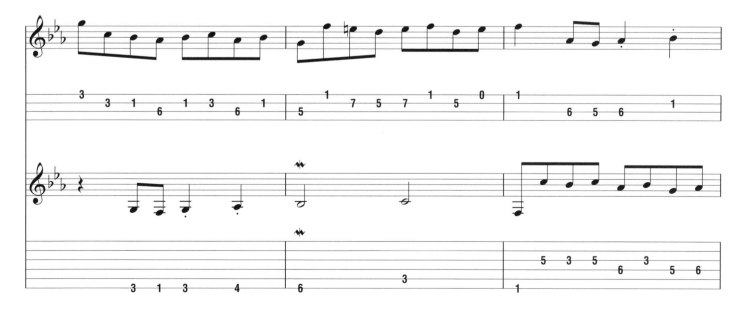

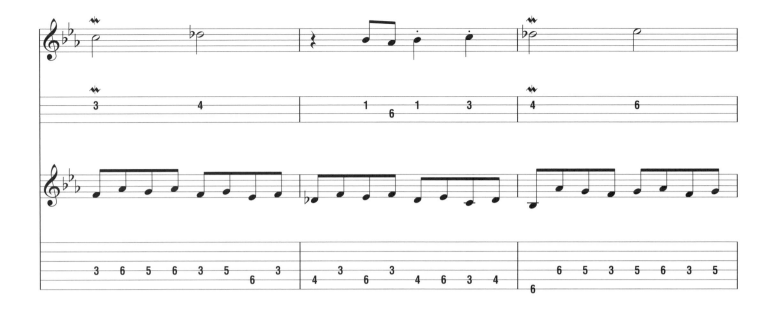

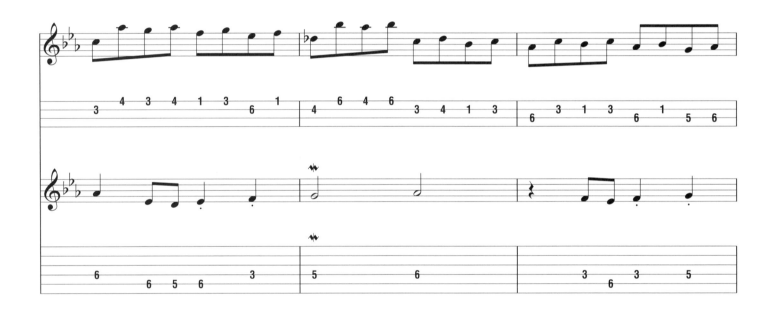

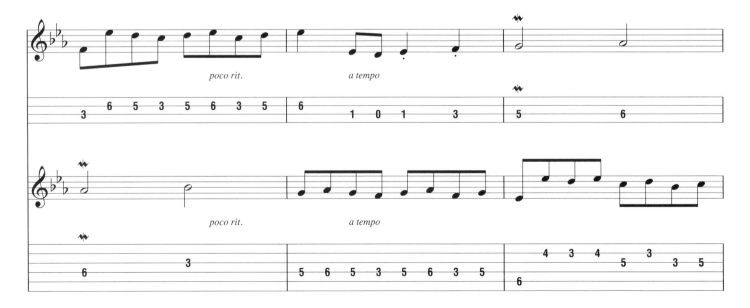

Invention No. 6

by Johann Sebastian Bach

Mandolin

Guitar

Invention No. 7

by Johann Sebastian Bach

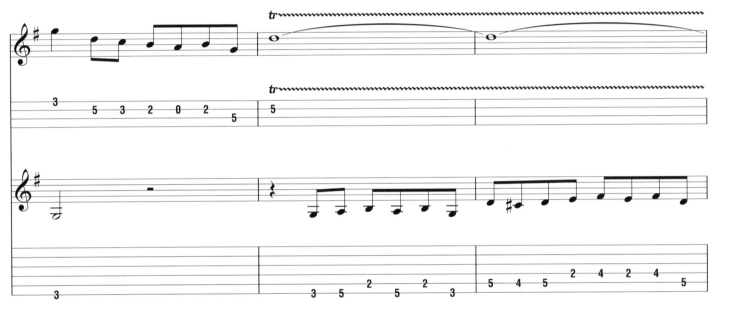

Bach Two-Part Inventions
FOR MANDOLIN & GUITAR
ARRANGED BY CARLO AONZO AND JOHN CARLINI

Invention No. 1

by Johann Sebastian Bach

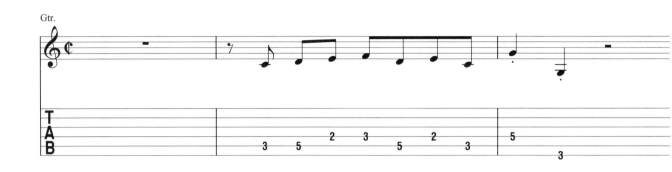

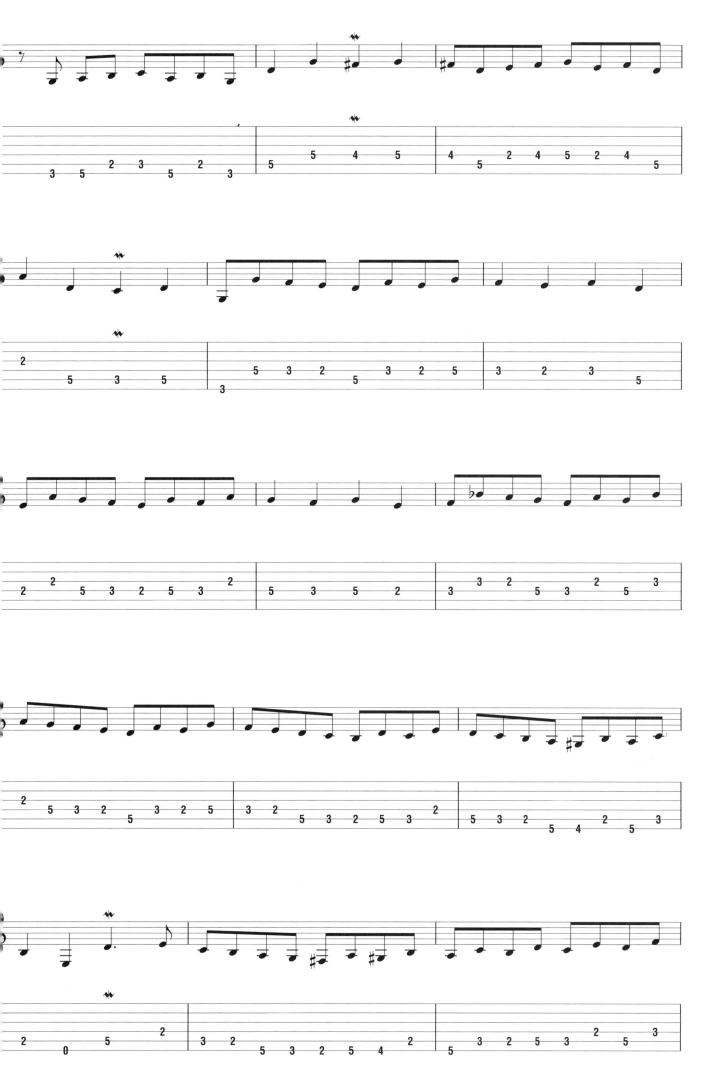

3

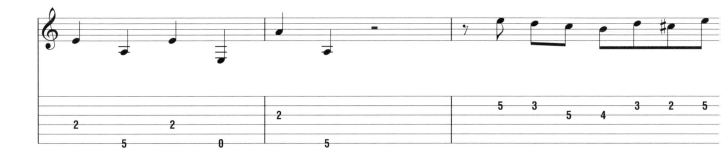

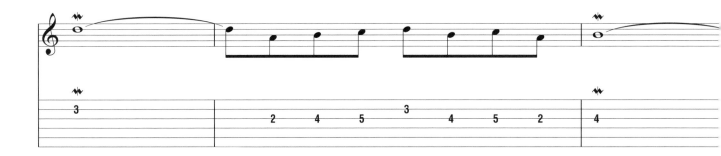

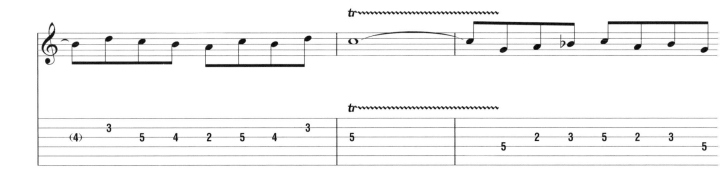

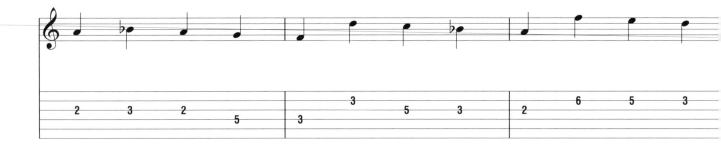

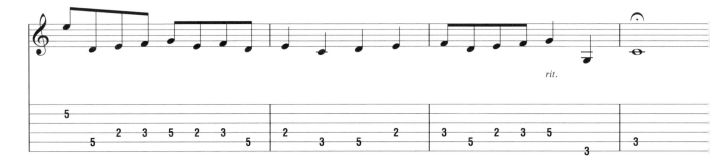

4

Invention No. 2

by Johann Sebastian Bach

Invention No. 3

by Johann Sebastian Bach

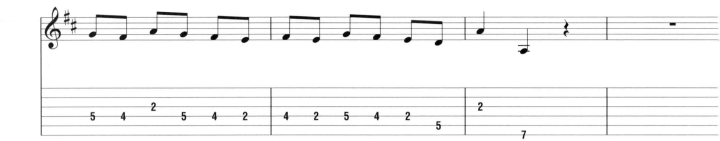

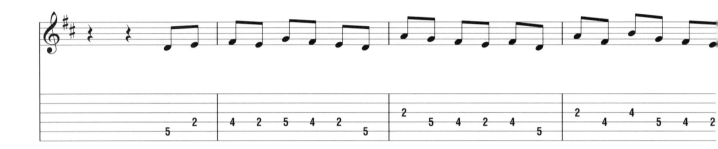

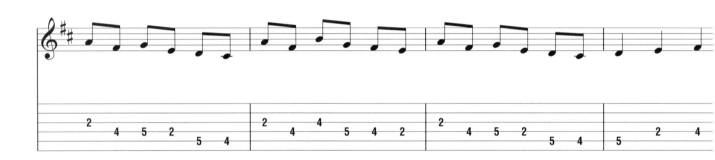

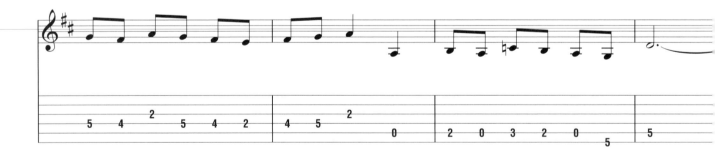

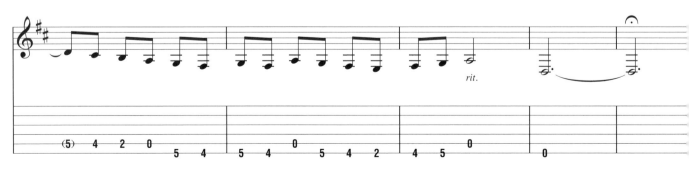

Invention No. 4

by Johann Sebastian Bach

Invention No. 5

by Johann Sebastian Bach

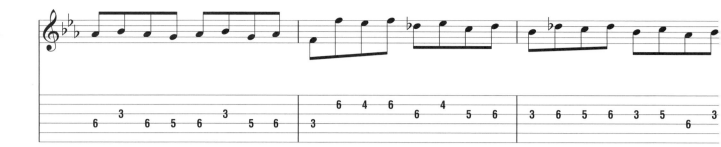

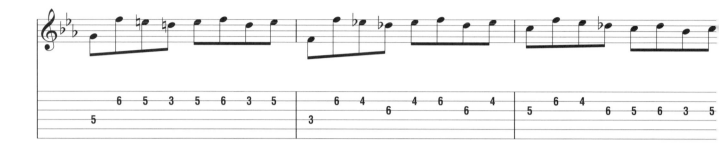

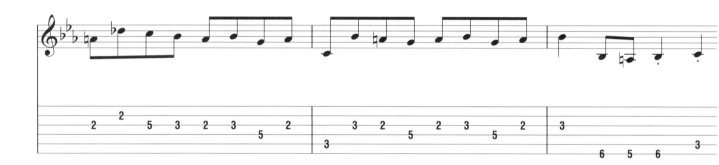

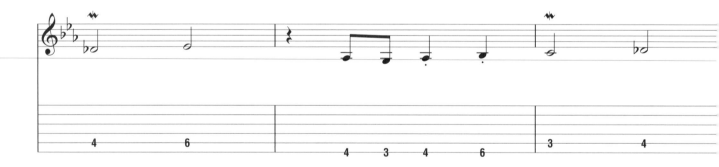

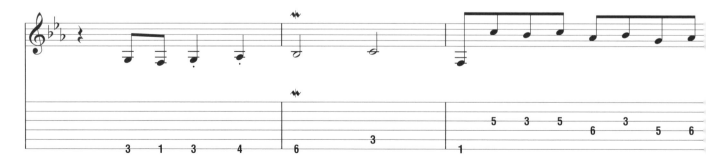

Invention No. 6

by Johann Sebastian Bach

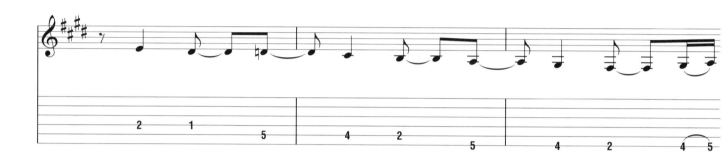

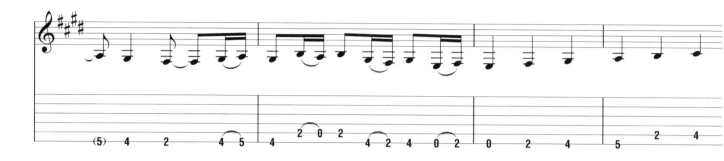

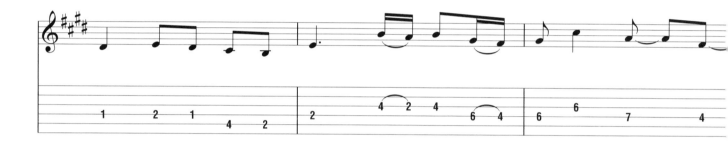

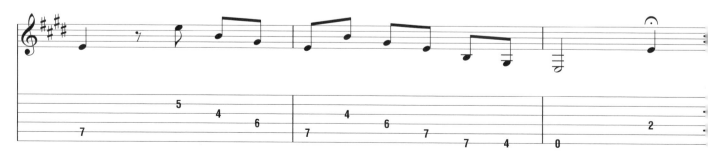

Invention No. 7

by Johann Sebastian Bach

22

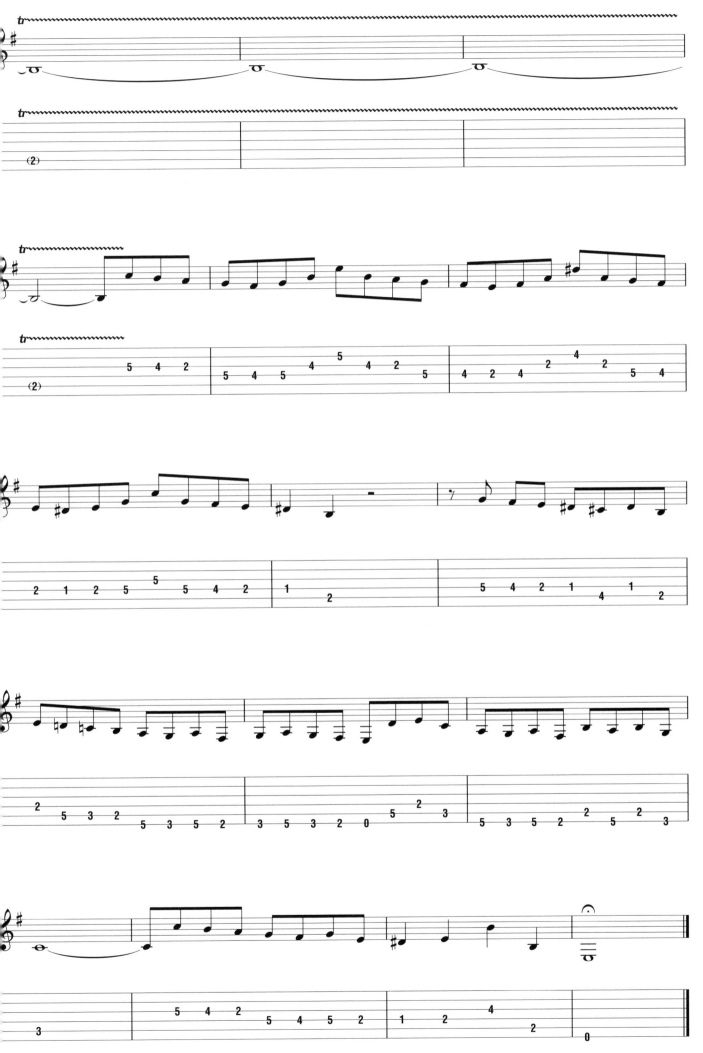

Invention No. 8

by Johann Sebastian Bach

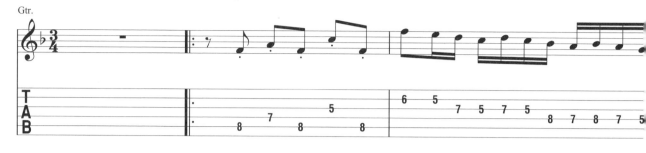

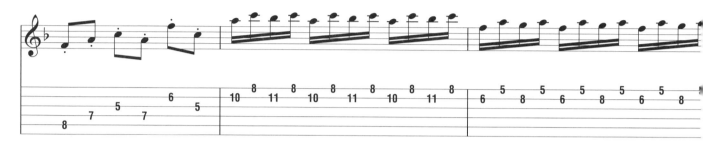

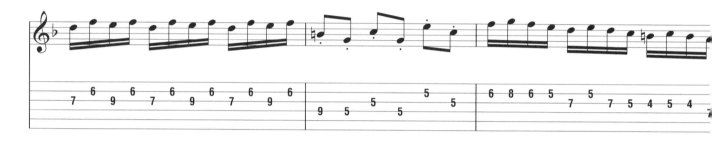

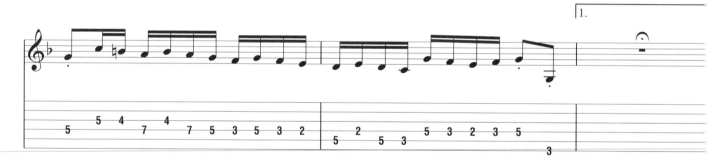

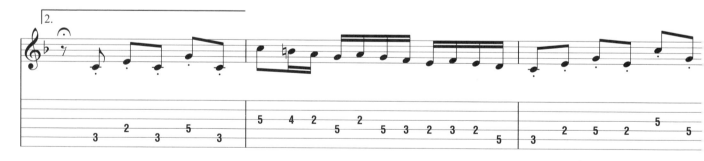

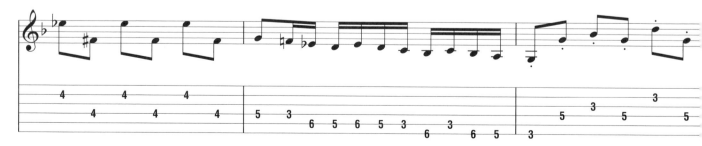

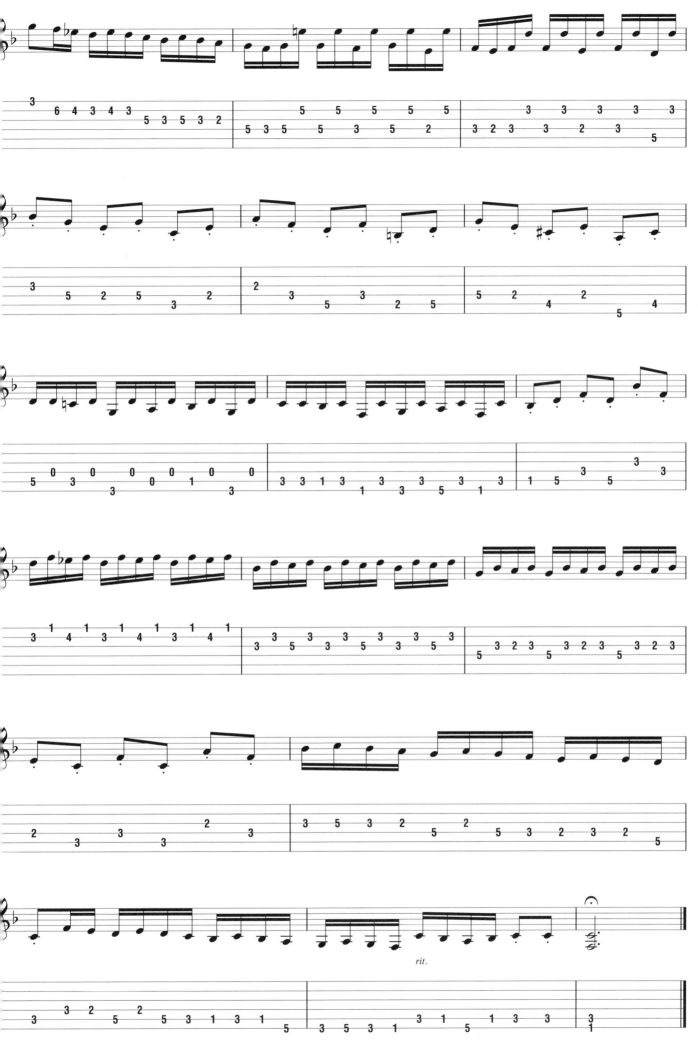

Invention No. 9

by Johann Sebastian Bach

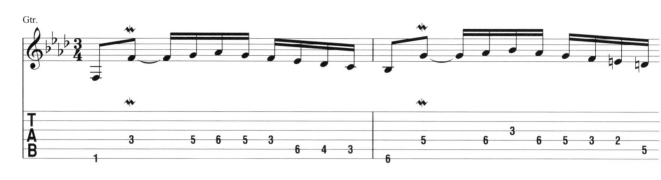

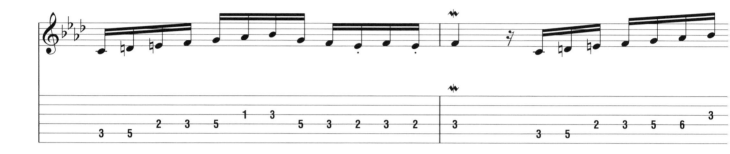

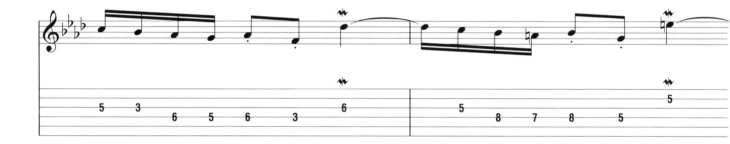

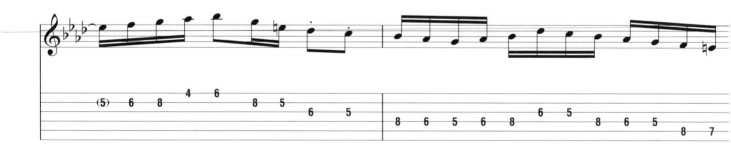

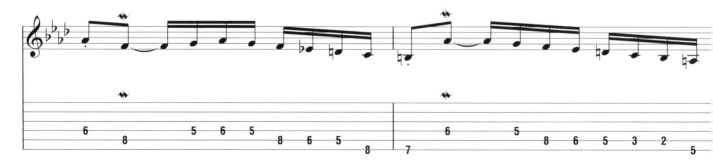

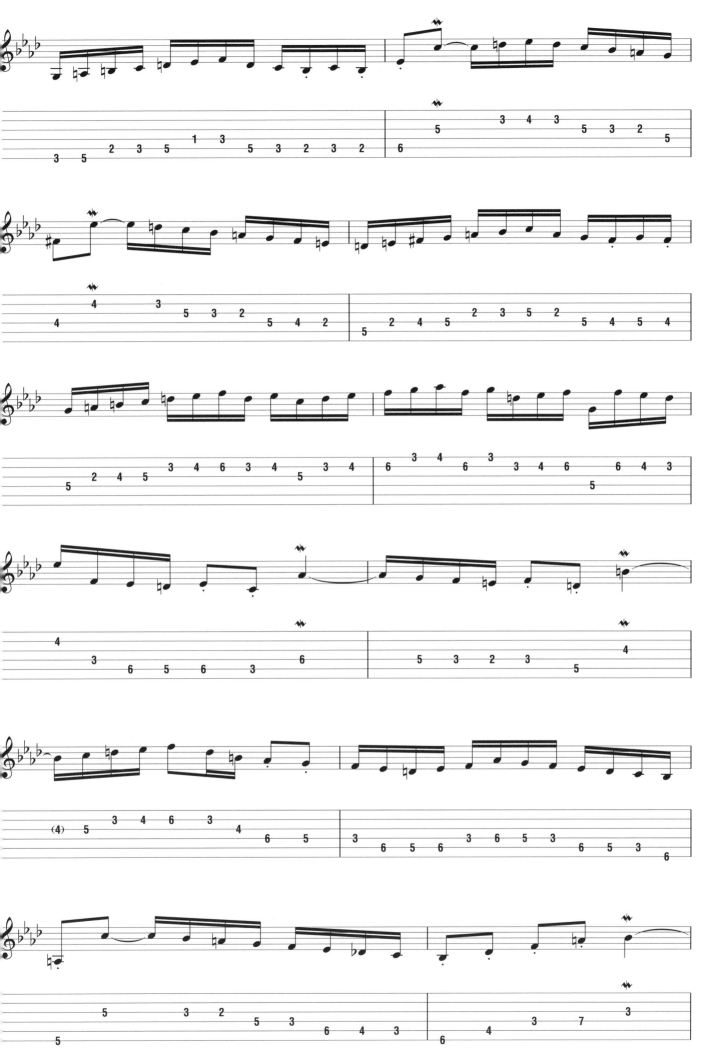

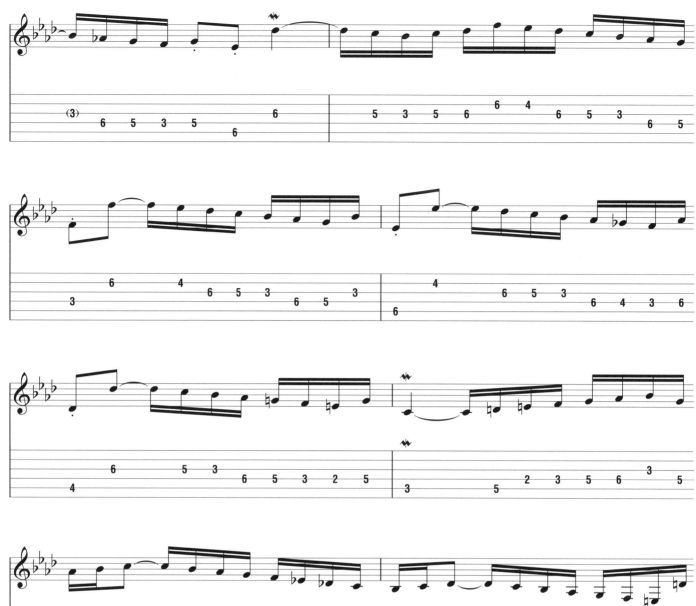

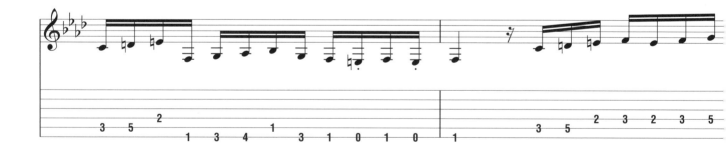

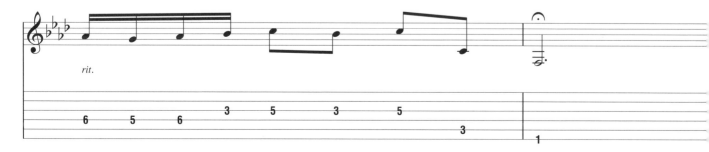

Invention No. 10

by Johann Sebastian Bach

Invention No. 11

by Johann Sebastian Bach

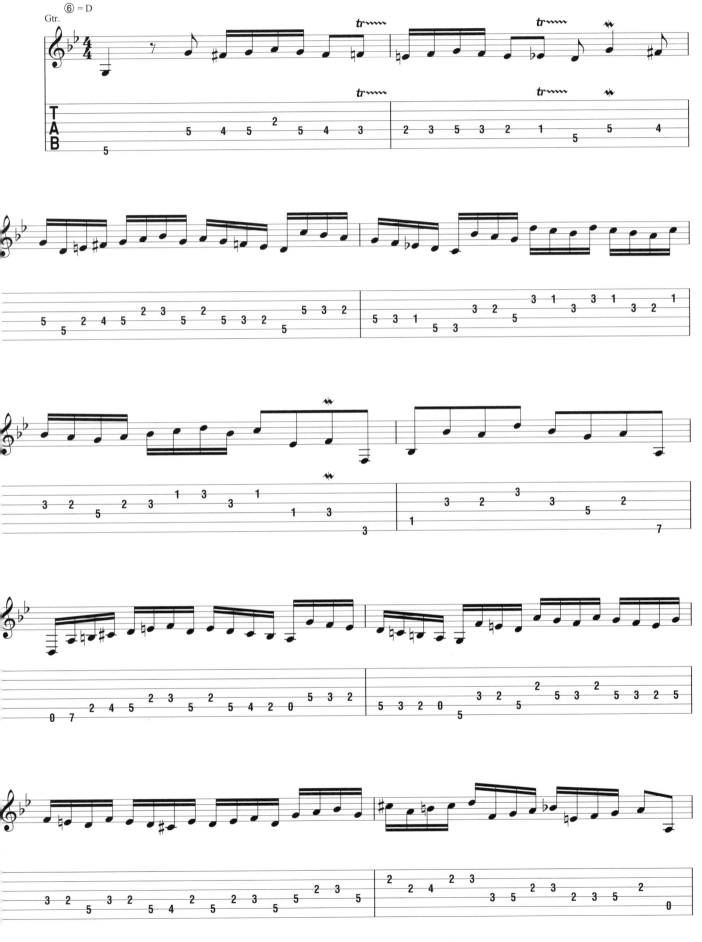

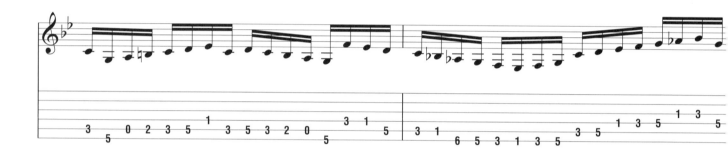

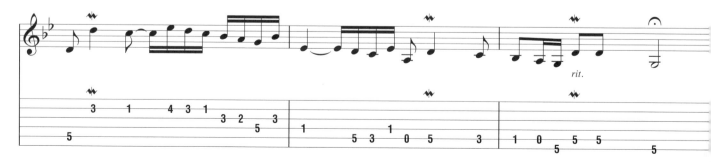

Invention No. 12

by Johann Sebastian Bach

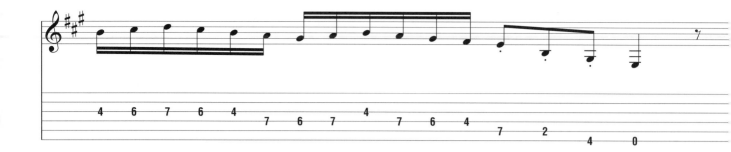

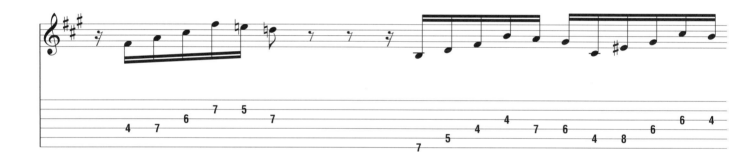

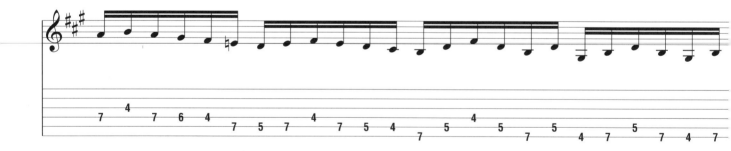

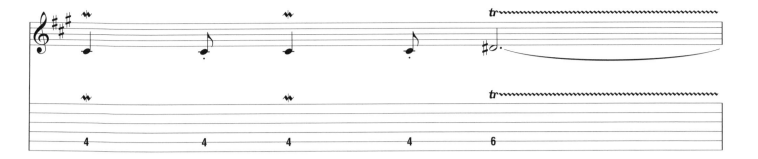

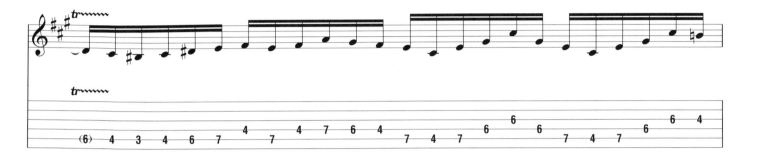

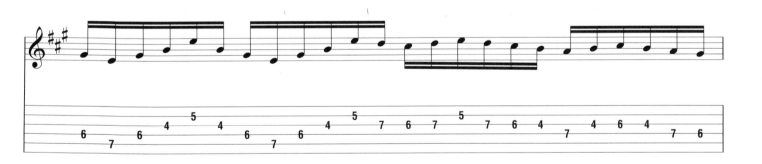

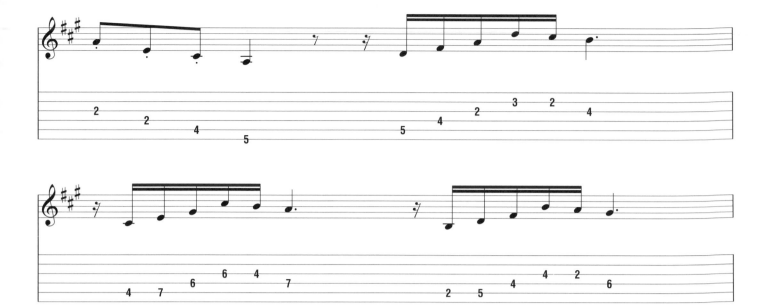

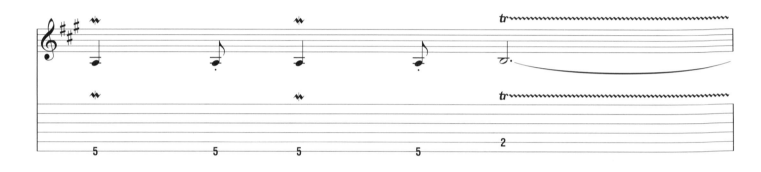

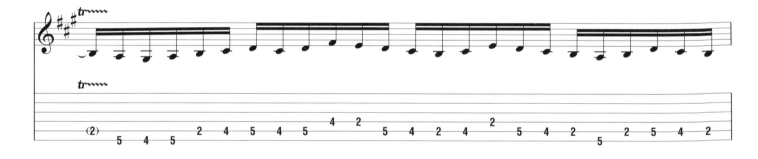

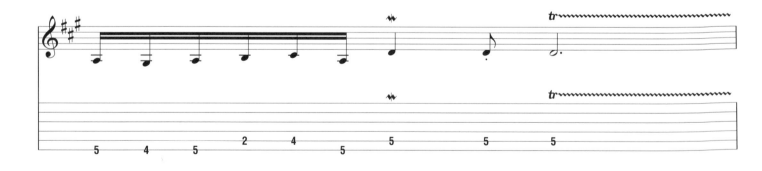

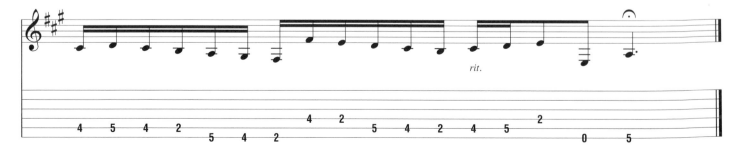

Invention No. 13

by Johann Sebastian Bach

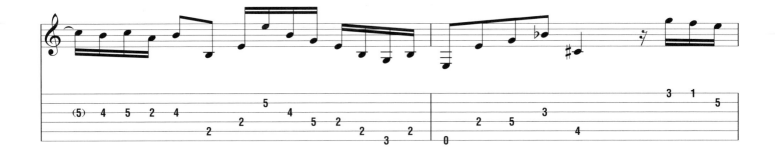

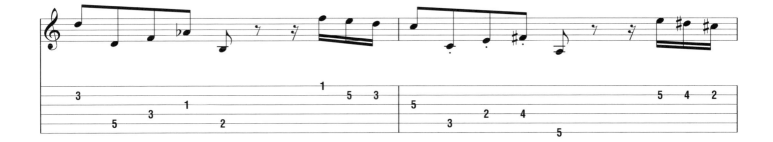

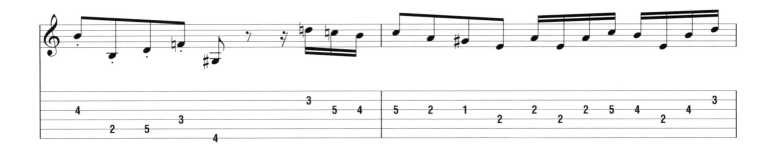

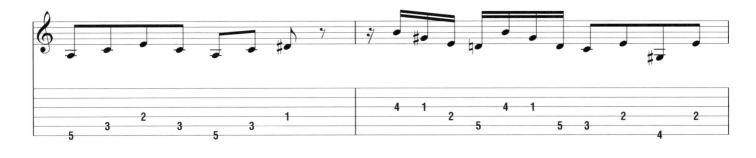

Invention No. 14

by Johann Sebastian Bach

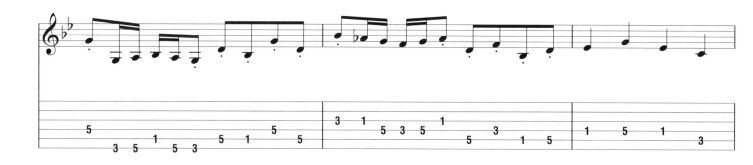

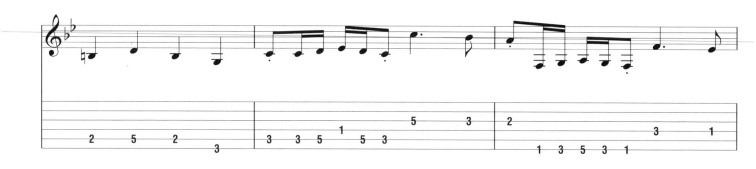

Invention No. 15

by Johann Sebastian Bach

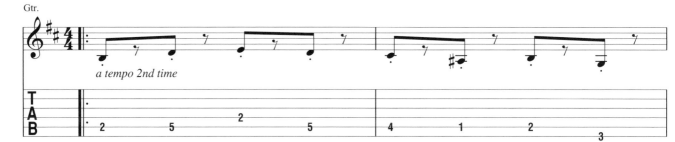

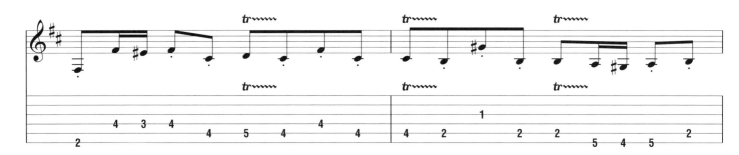

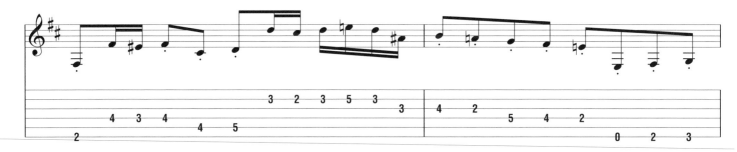

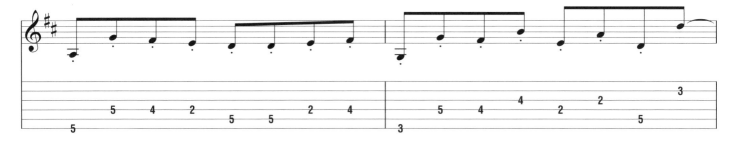

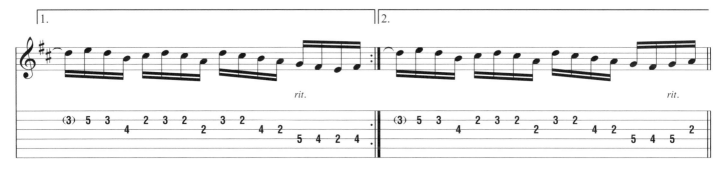

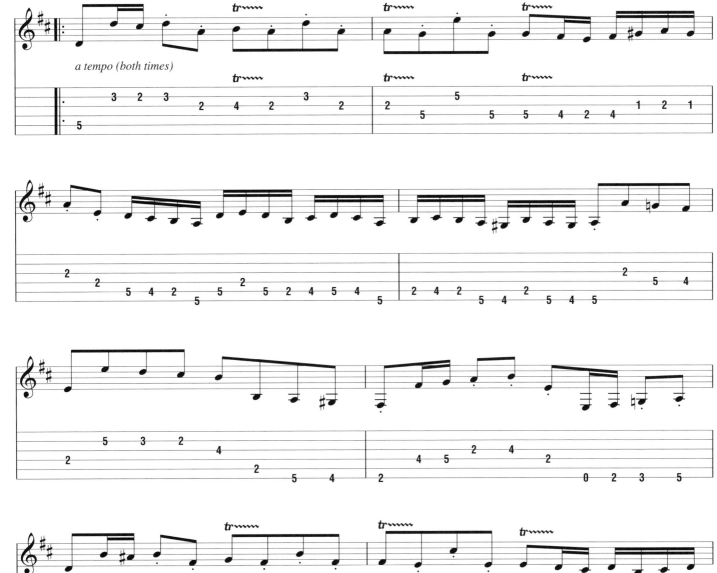

a tempo (both times)

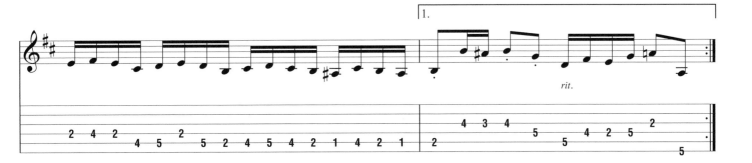

rit.

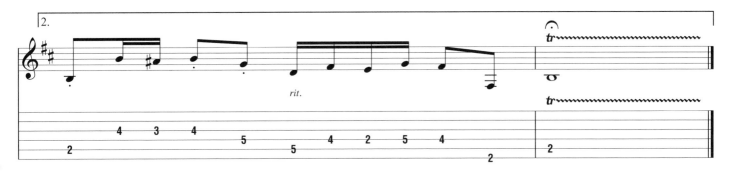

rit.

Bach Two-Part Inventions
FOR MANDOLIN & GUITAR

ARRANGED BY CARLO AONZO AND JOHN CARLINI

Invention No. 1

by Johann Sebastian Bach

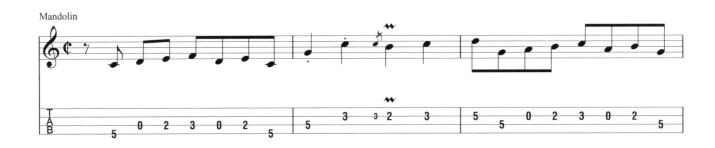

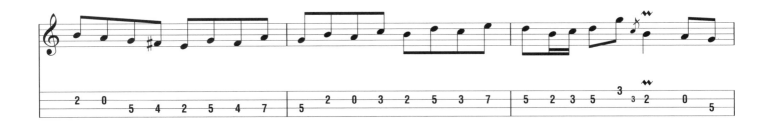

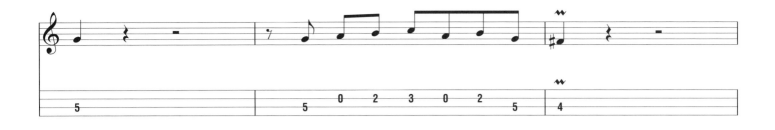

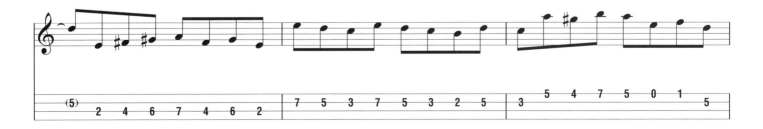

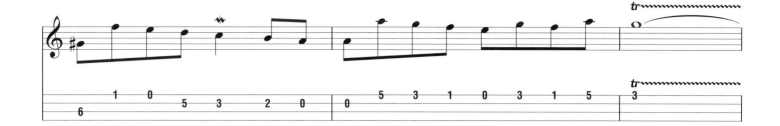

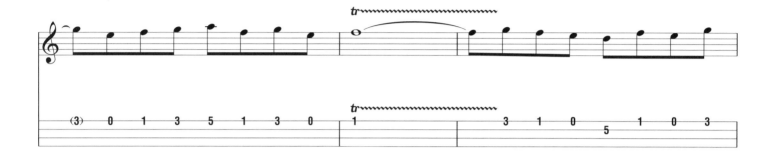

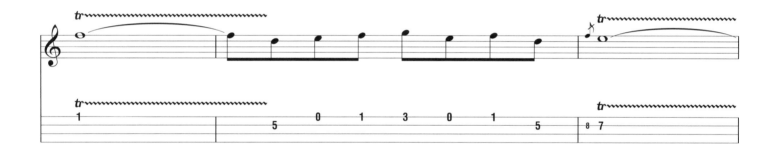

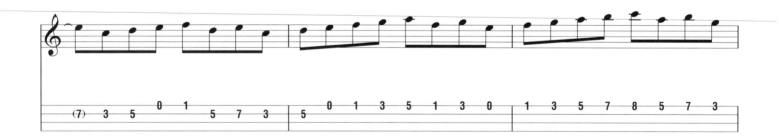

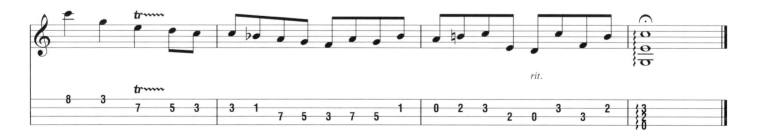

Invention No. 2

by Johann Sebastian Bach

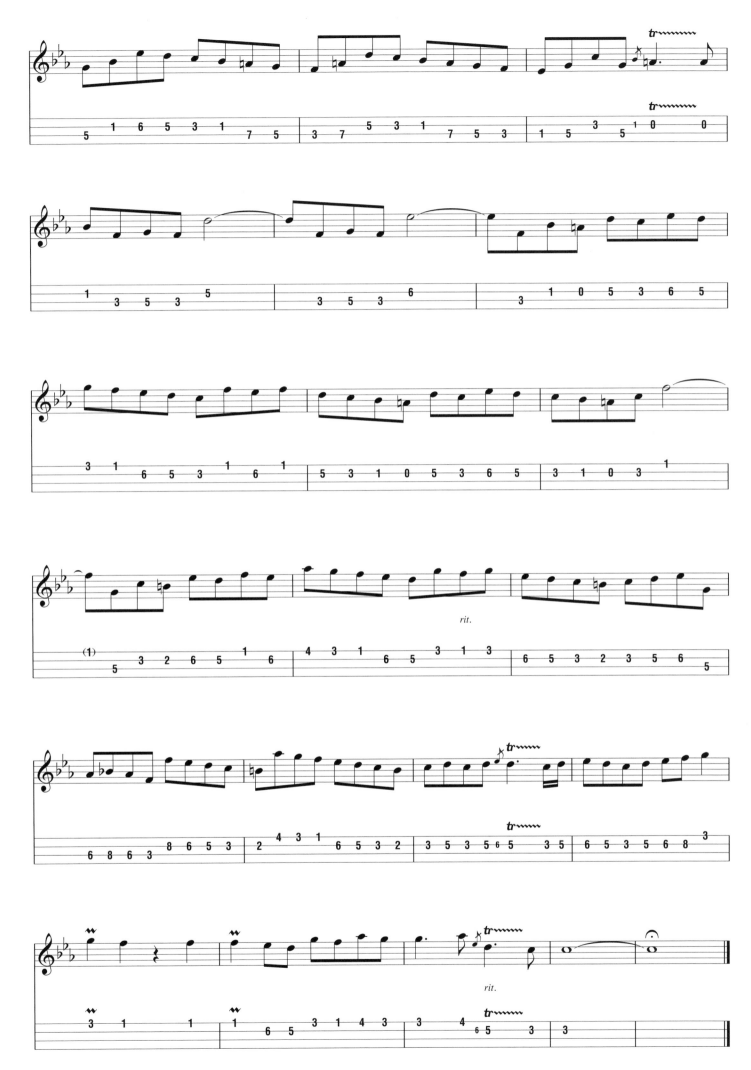

Invention No. 3

by Johann Sebastian Bach

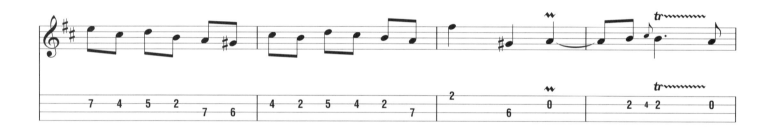

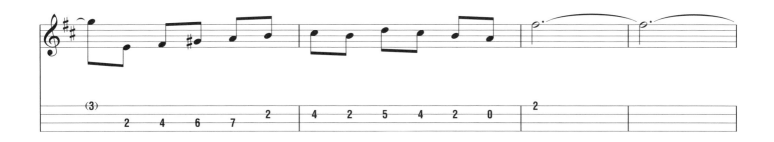

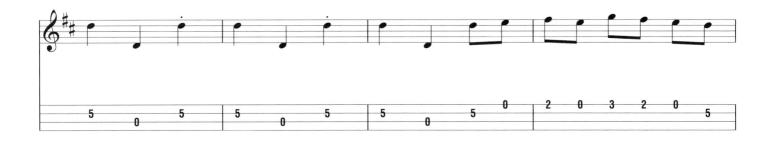

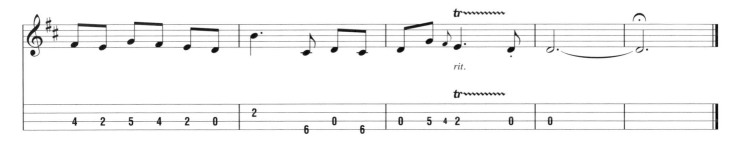

Invention No. 4

by Johann Sebastian Bach

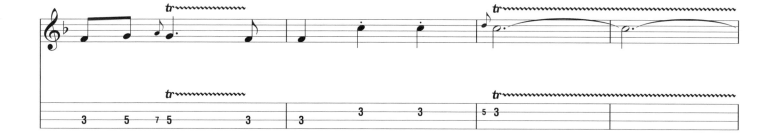

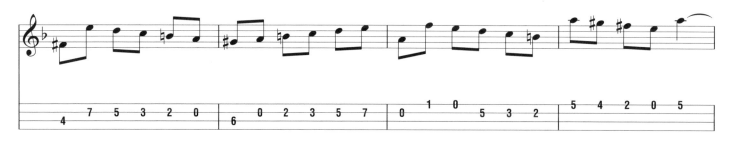

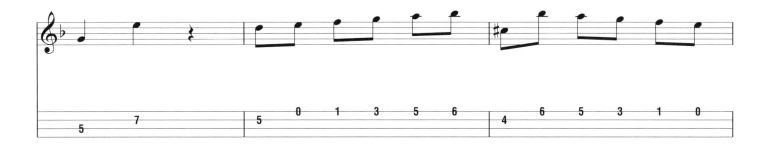

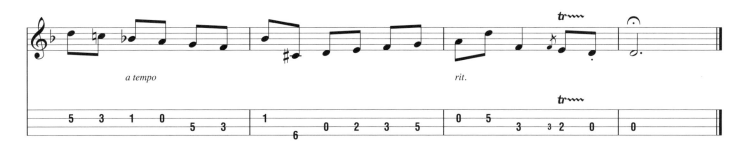

Invention No. 5

by Johann Sebastian Bach

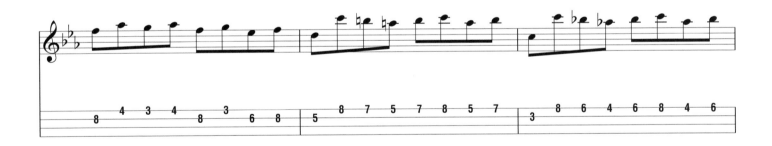

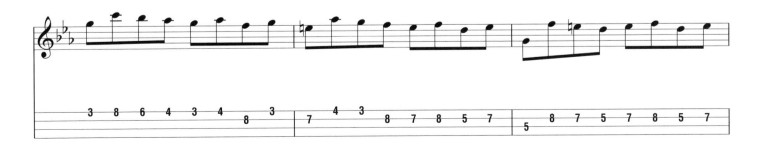

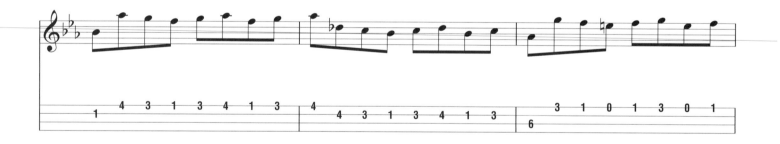

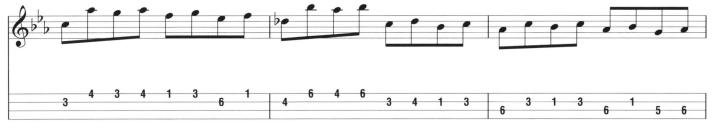

poco rit.   *a tempo*

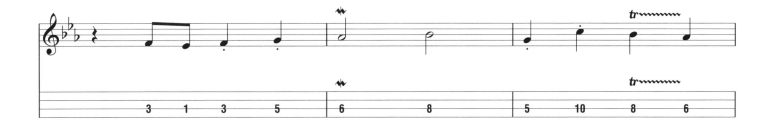

rit.

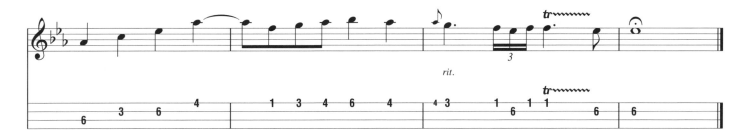

Invention No. 6

by Johann Sebastian Bach

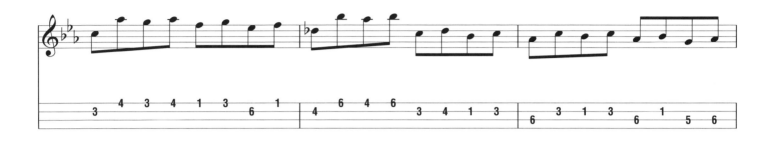

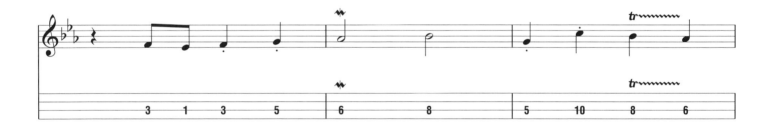

Invention No. 6

by Johann Sebastian Bach

19

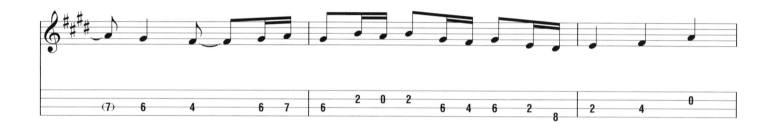

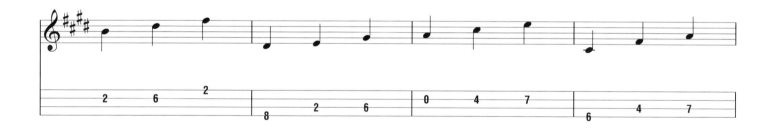

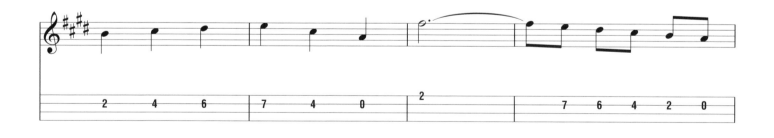

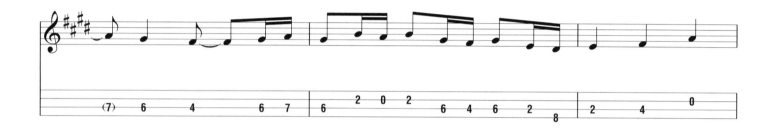

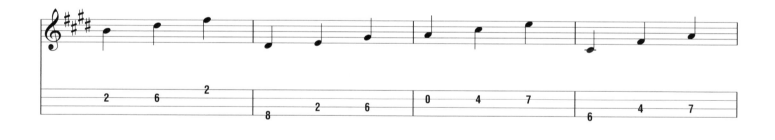

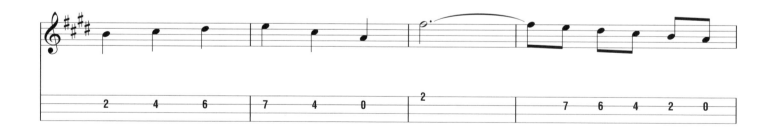

Invention No. 7

by Johann Sebastian Bach

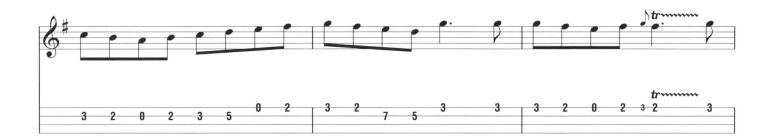

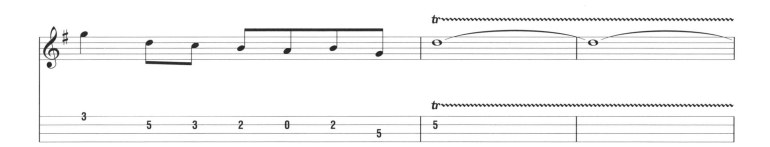

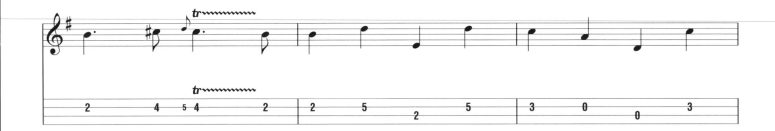

Invention No. 8

by Johann Sebastian Bach

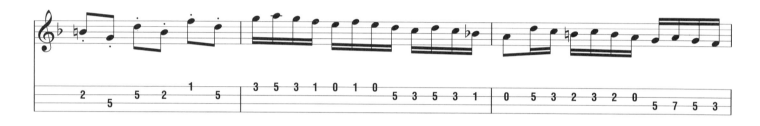

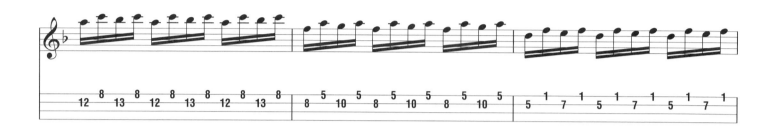

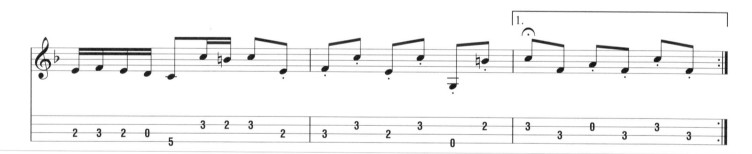

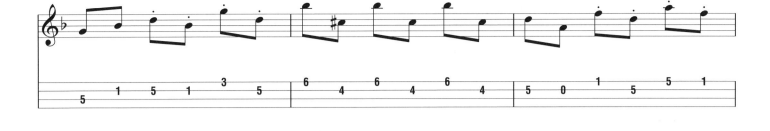

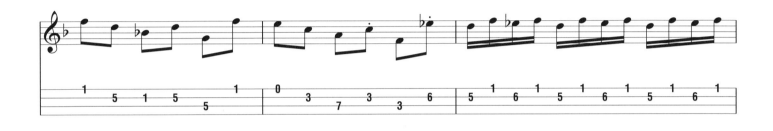

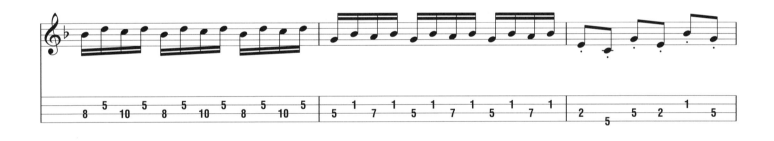

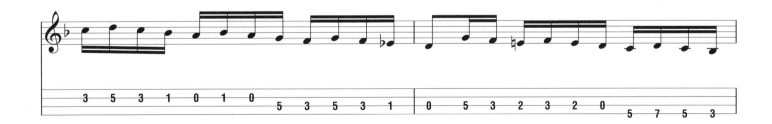

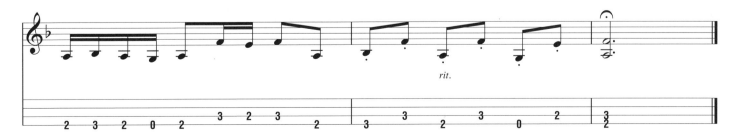

25

Invention No. 9

by Johann Sebastian Bach

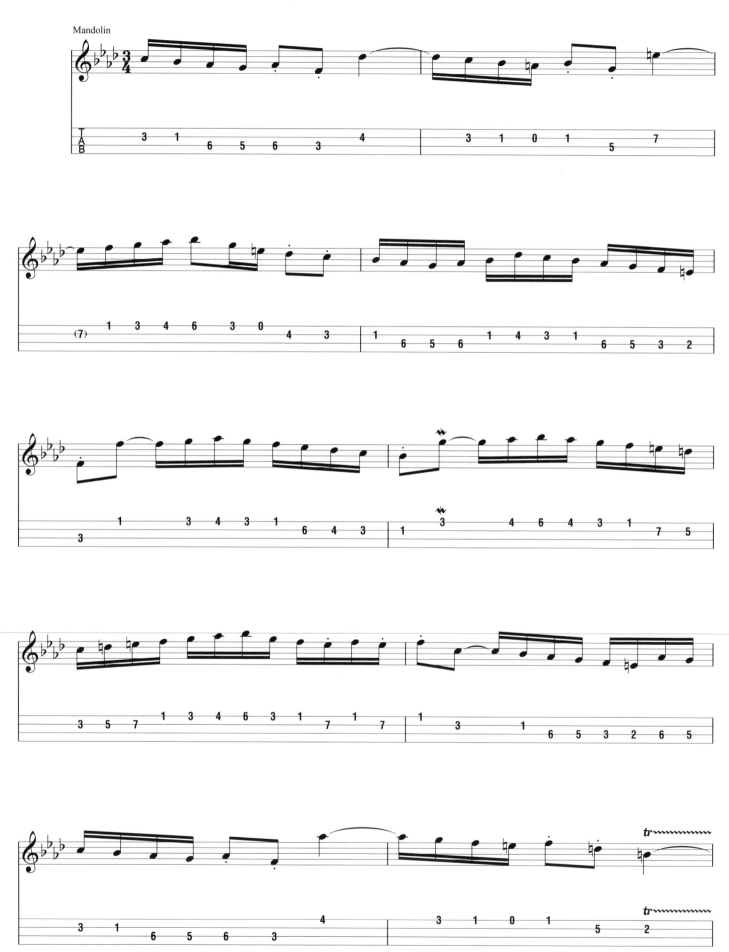

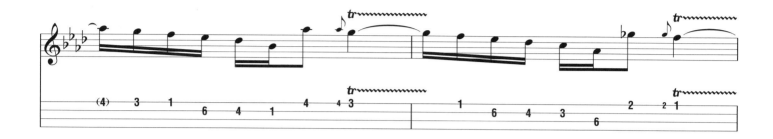

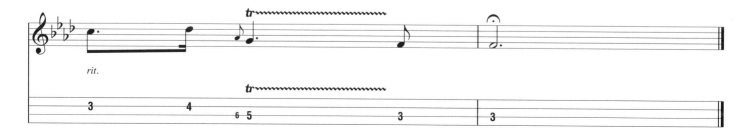

Invention No. 10

by Johann Sebastian Bach

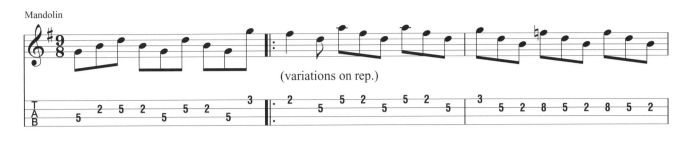

(variations on rep.)

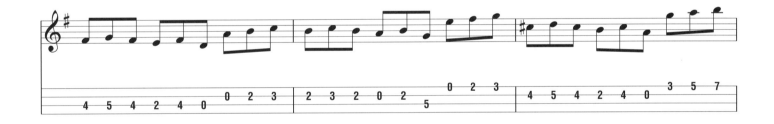

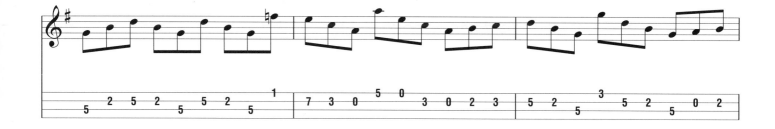

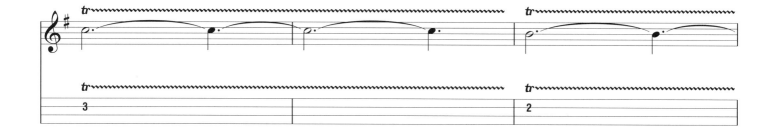

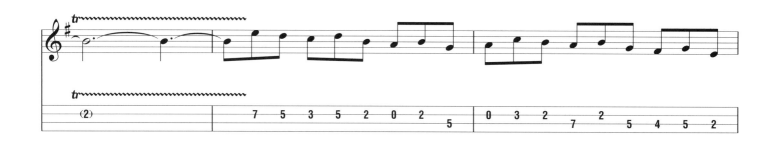

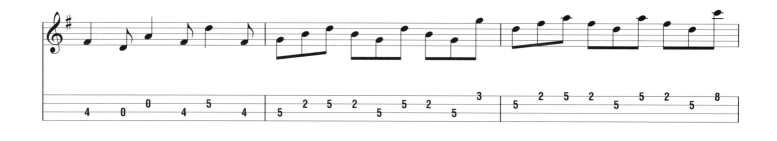

Invention No. 11

by Johann Sebastian Bach

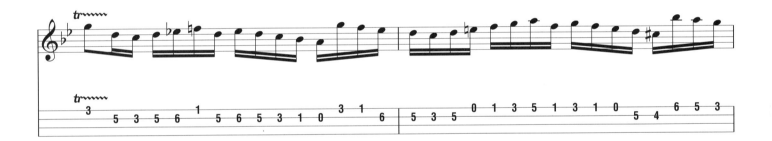

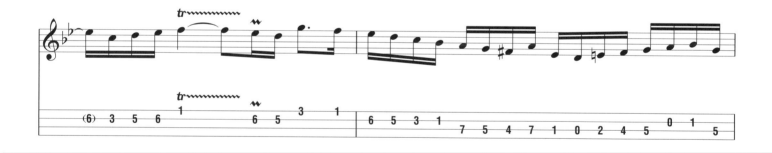

Invention No. 12

by Johann Sebastian Bach

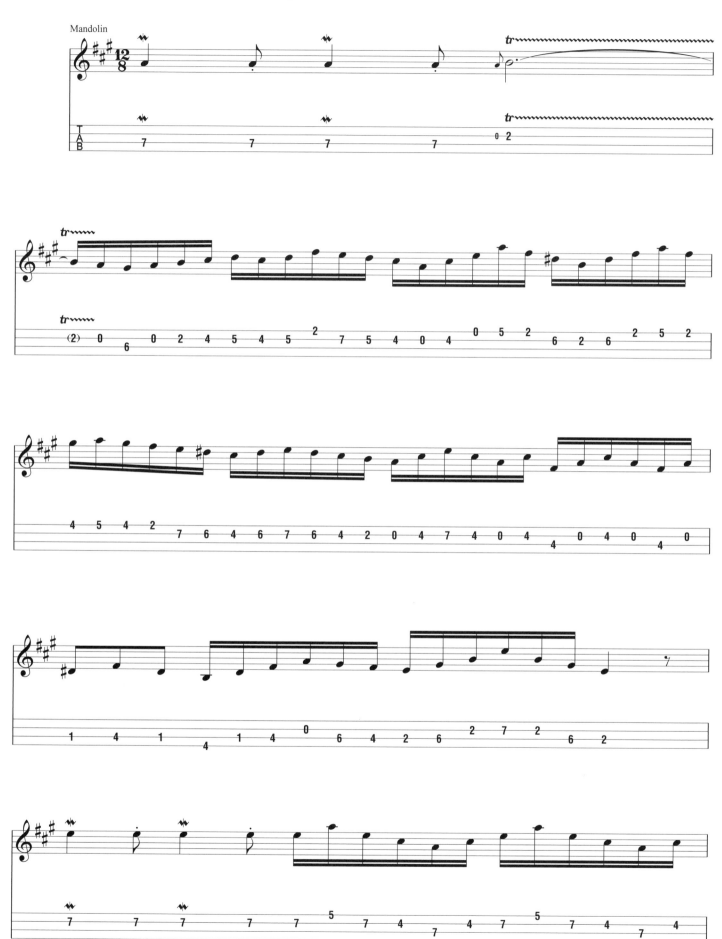

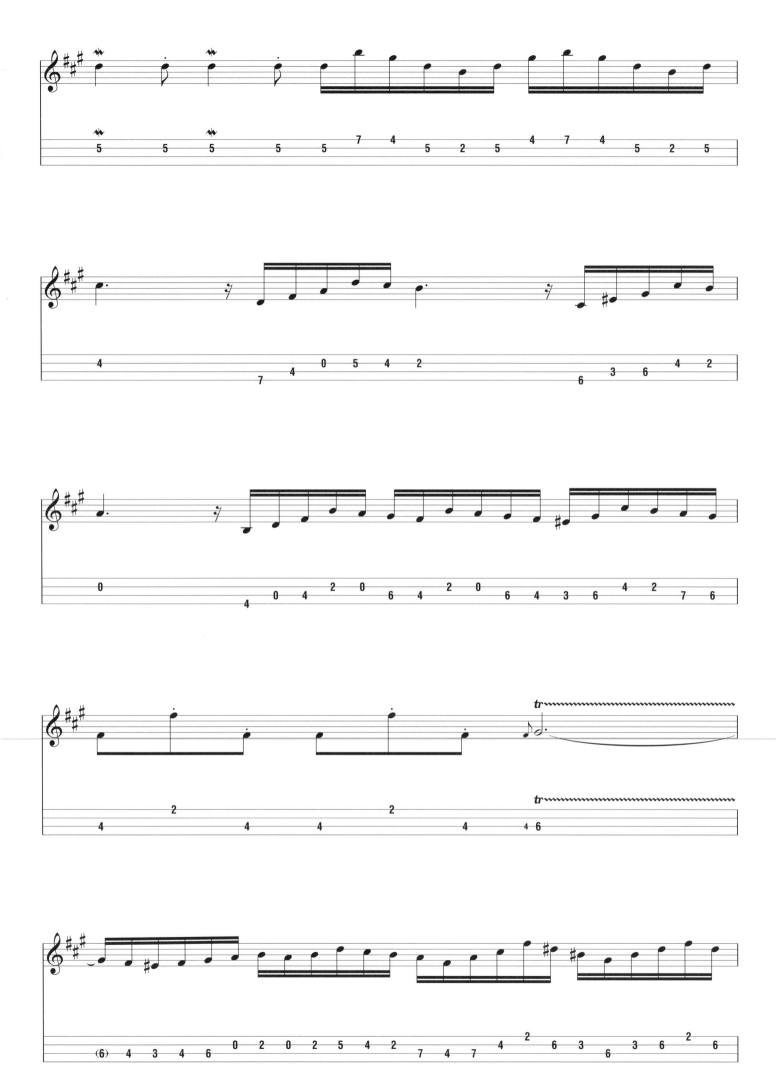

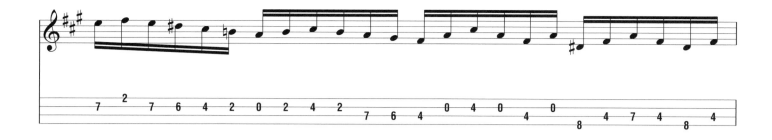

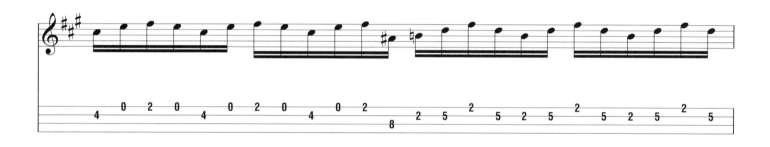

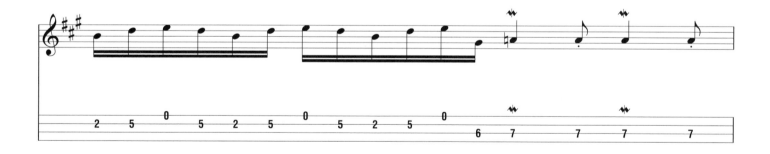

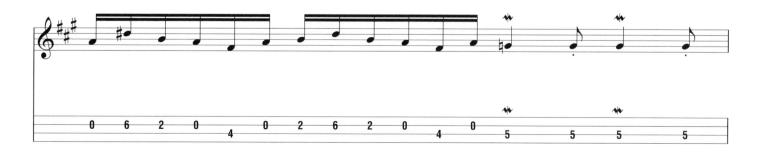

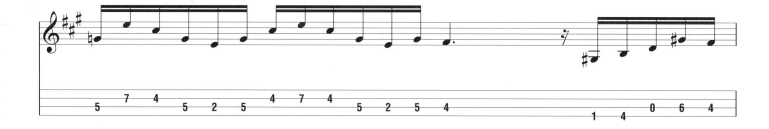

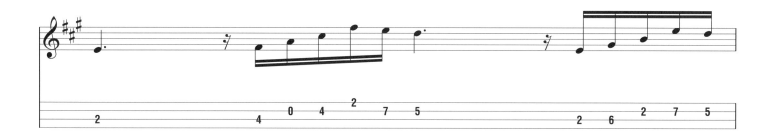

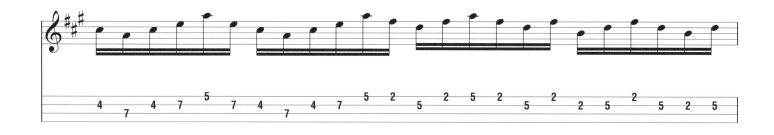

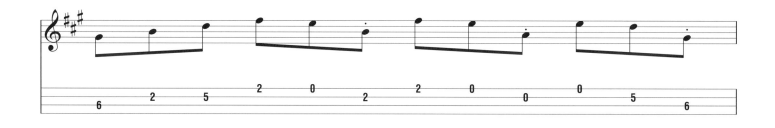

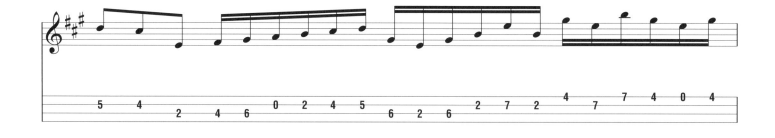

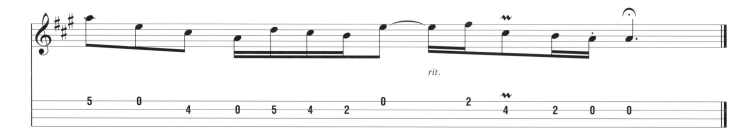

Invention No. 13

by Johann Sebastian Bach

Invention No. 14

by Johann Sebastian Bach

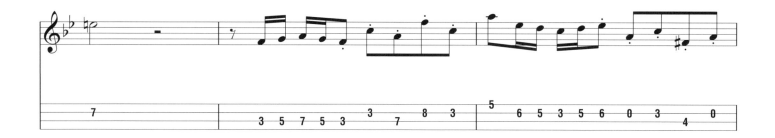

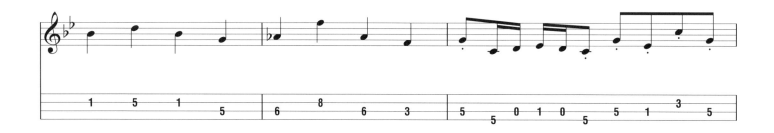

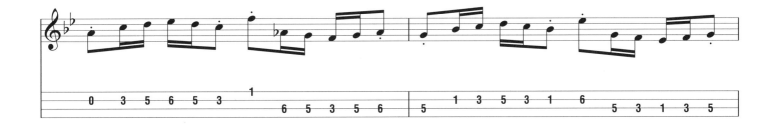

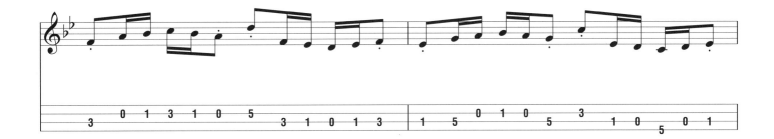

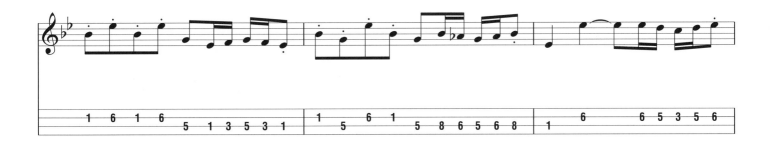

Invention No. 15

by Johann Sebastian Bach

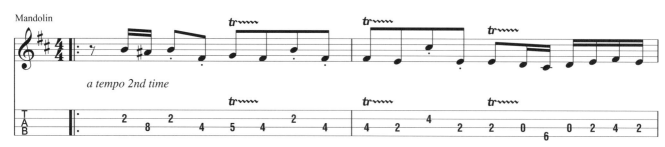

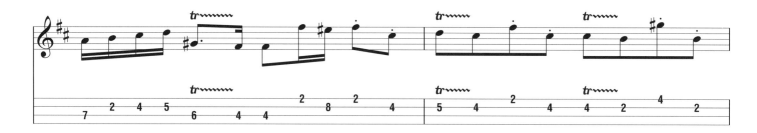

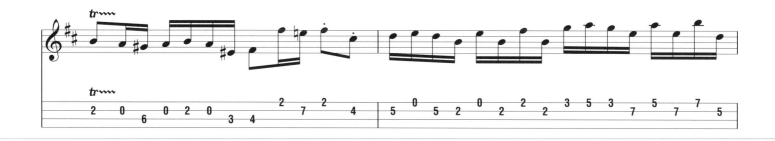

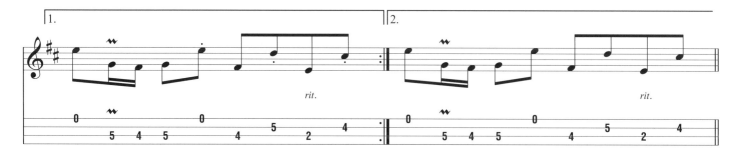

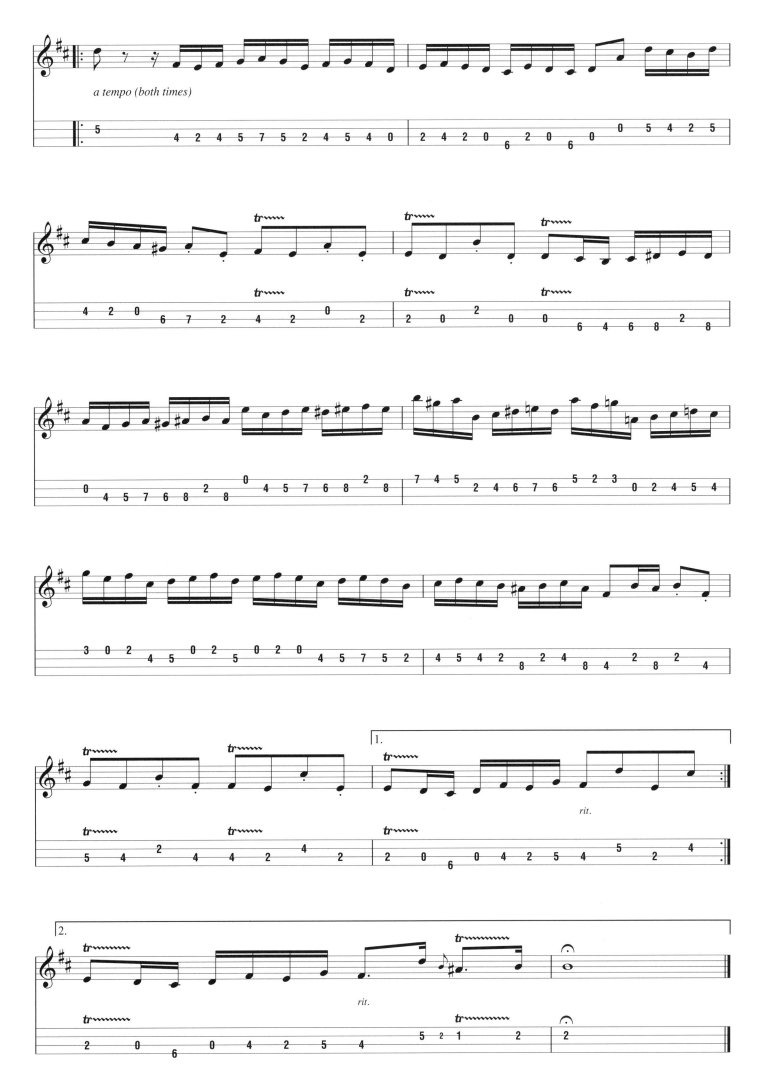

a tempo (both times)

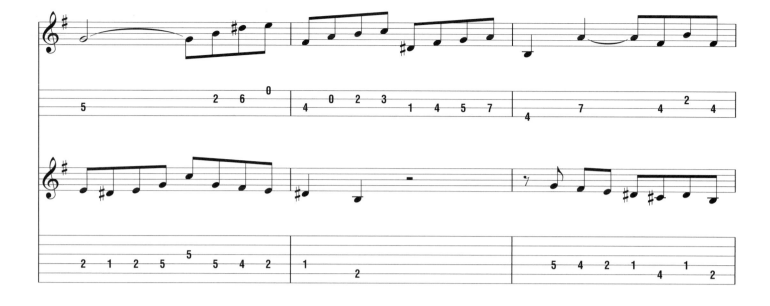

Invention No. 8

by Johann Sebastian Bach

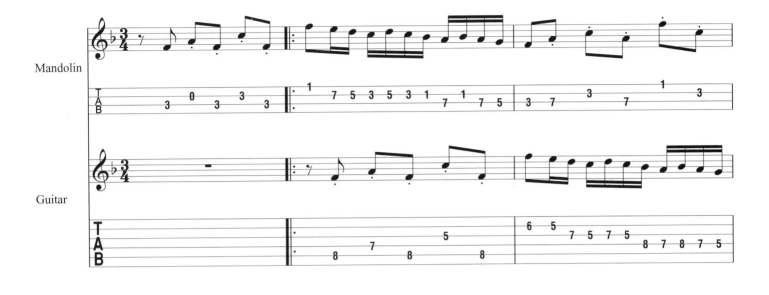

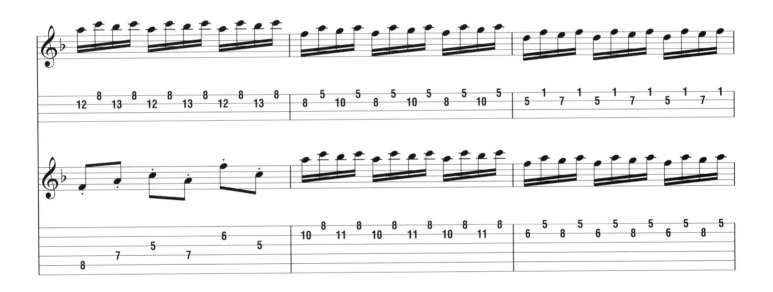

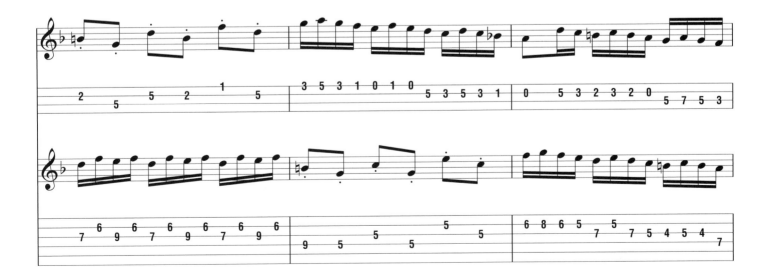

Invention No. 9

by Johann Sebastian Bach

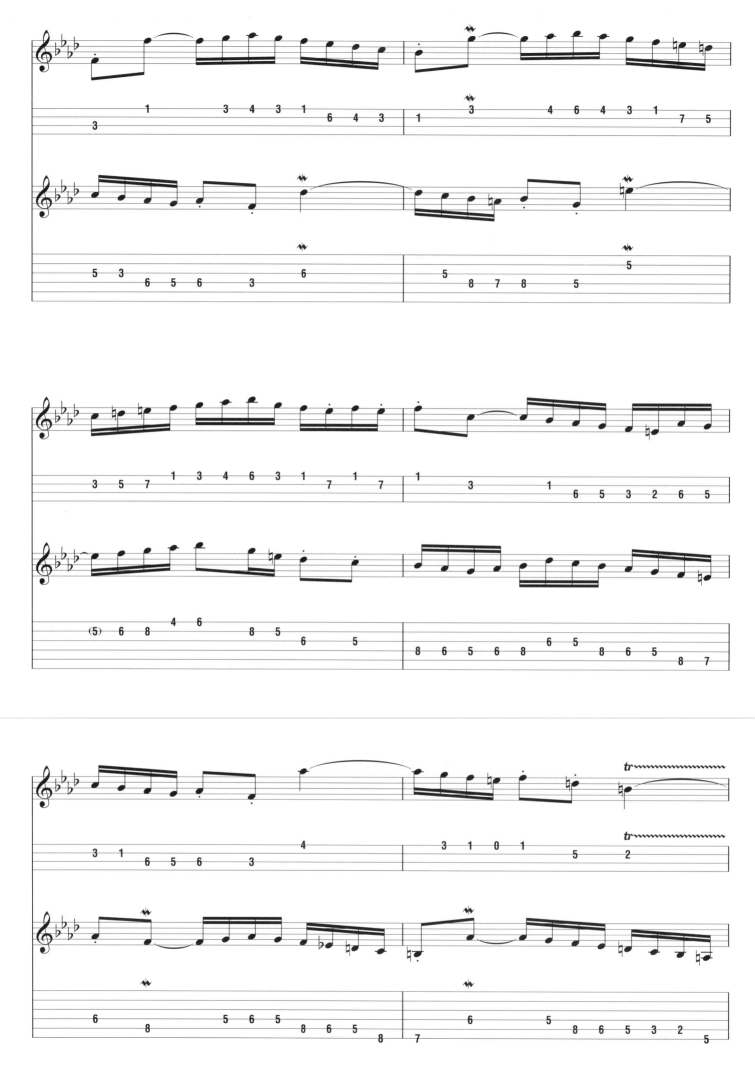

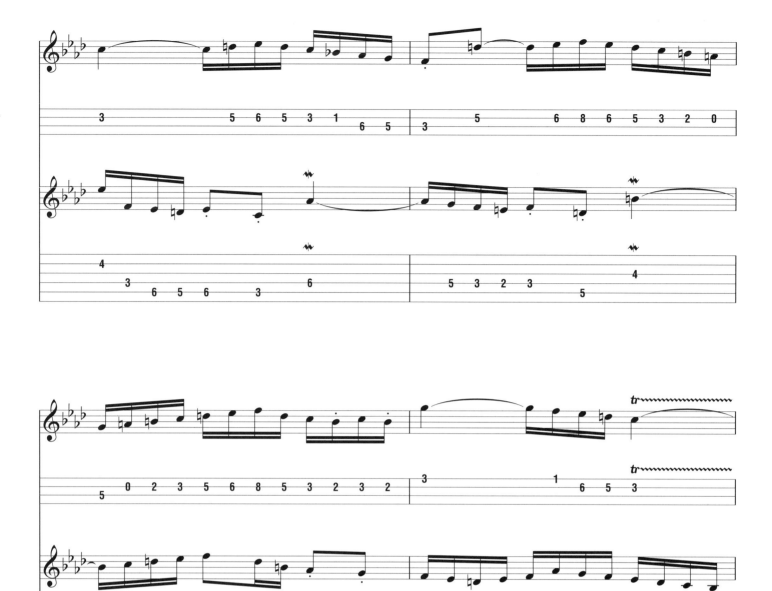

Invention No. 10

by Johann Sebastian Bach

Invention No. 11

by Johann Sebastian Bach

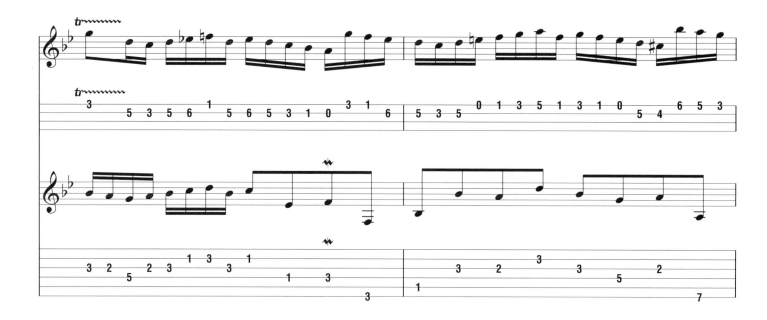

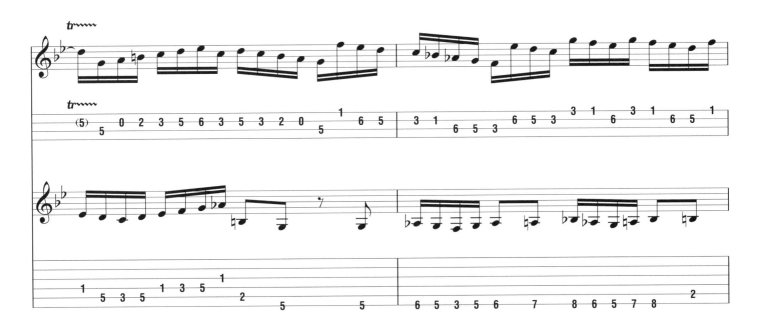

Invention No. 12

by Johann Sebastian Bach

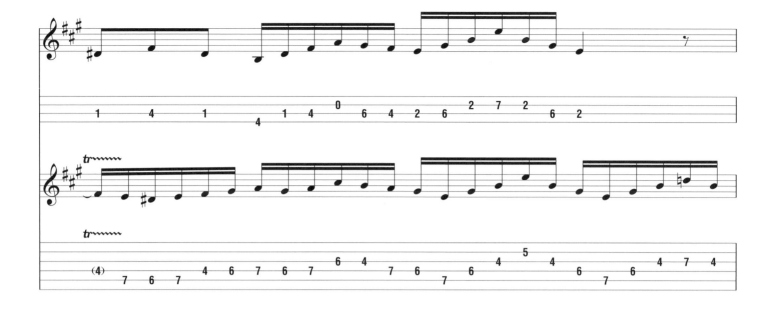

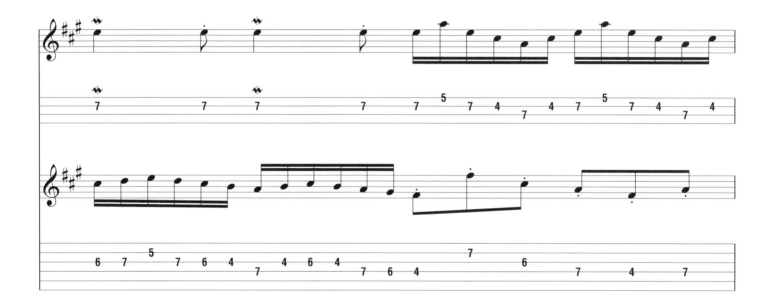

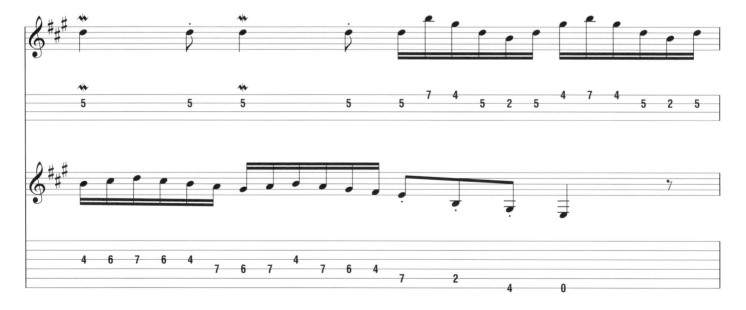

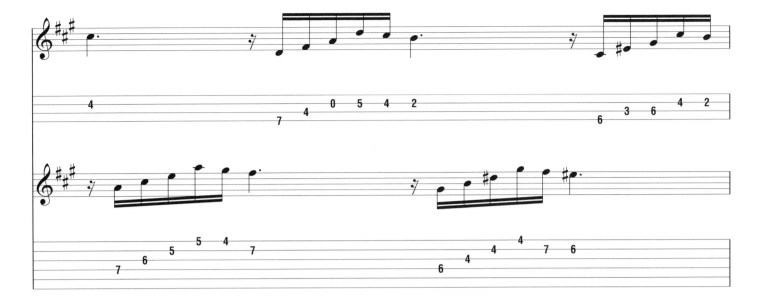

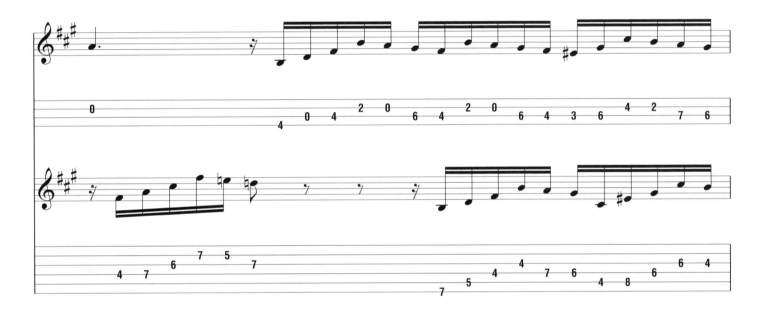

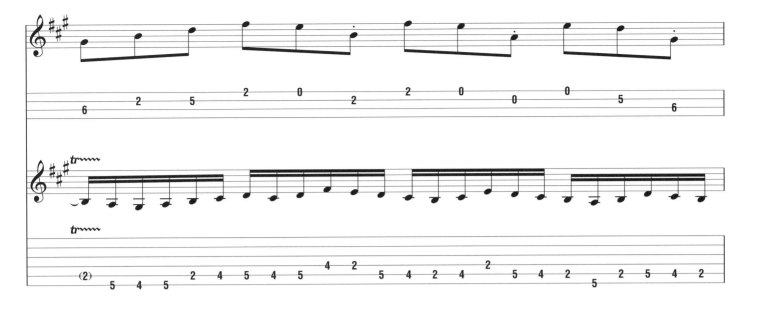

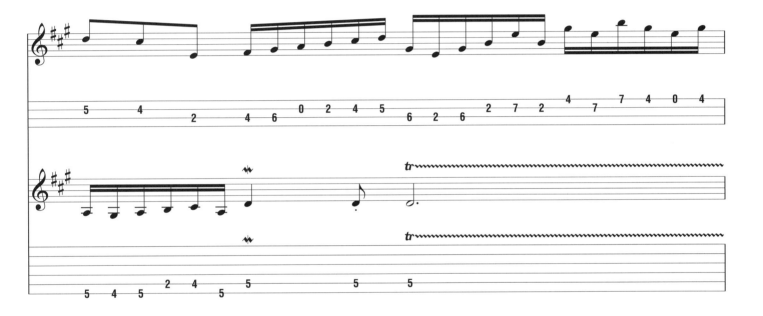

Invention No. 13

by Johann Sebastian Bach

Mandolin

Guitar

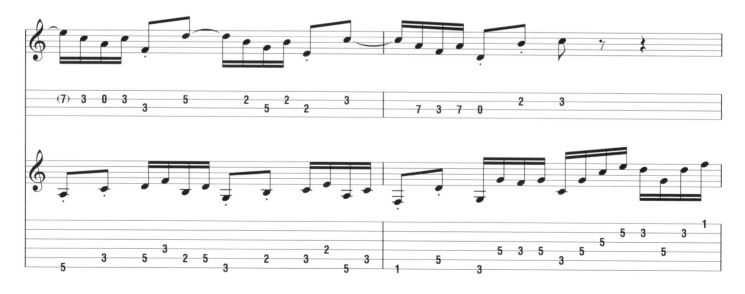

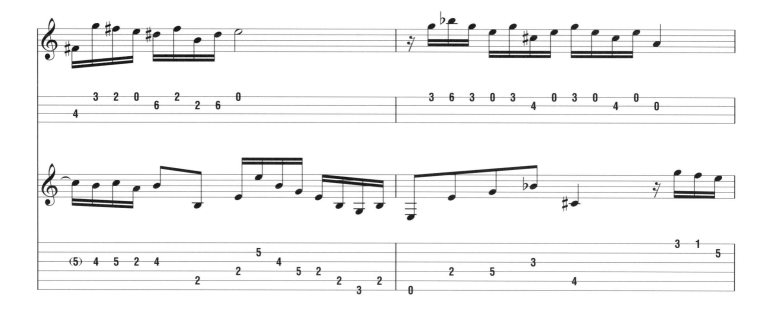

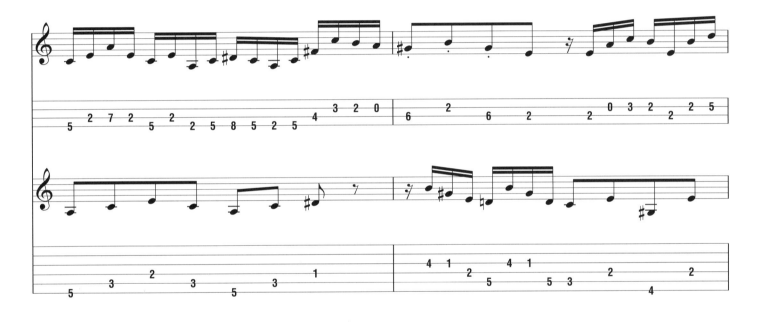

Invention No. 14

by Johann Sebastian Bach

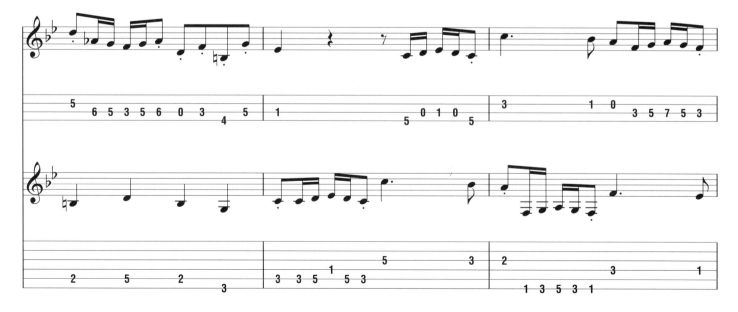

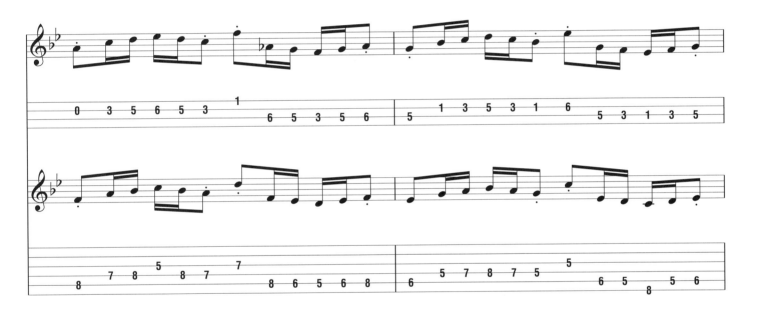

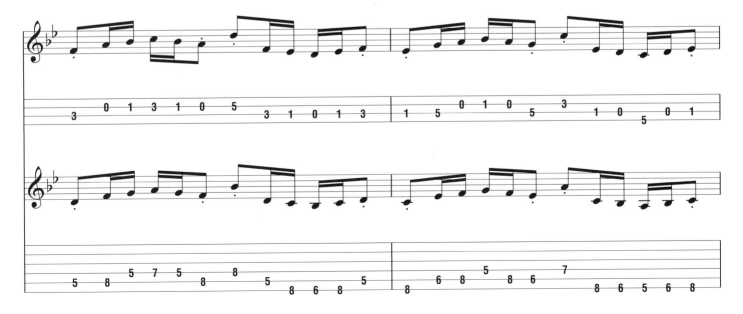

Invention No. 15

by Johann Sebastian Bach

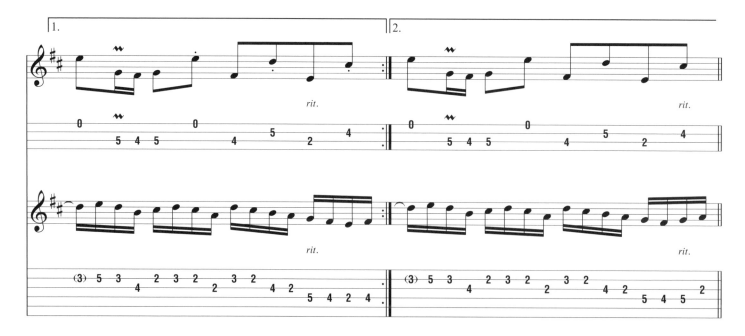

a tempo (both times)

a tempo (both times)